OVERCOMING A NARCISSISTIC RELATIONSHIP

A healing guide to overcoming the abuse of a narcissistic partner, learn how to increase your own self-esteem and deal with anxiety in toxic relationships.

by Grace Richards

Disclaimer

All erudition supplied in this book is specified for educational and academic purposes only. The author is not in any way in charge of any results that emerge from utilizing this book. Constructive efforts have been made to render information that is both precise and effective. Still, the author is not to be held answerable for the accuracy or use/misuse of this information.

Foreword

I will like to thank you for taking the very first step of trusting me and deciding to purchase/read this life-transforming book. Thanks for investing your time and resources on this product.

I can assure you of precise outcomes if you will diligently follow the specific blueprint I lay bare in the information handbook you are currently checking out. It has transformed lives, and I firmly believe it will equally change your own life too.

All the information I provided in this *Do It Yourself* piece is easy to absorb and practice.

Table of Contents

INTRODUCTION

Finding yourself involved with a narcissist is an adventure, that's for sure. It will open your eyes to human nature, our broken society, and, perhaps most importantly, your spirit. It's a dark journey that will toss you into spells of anxiety, loneliness, and rage. It will decipher your inner insecurities, leaving you with a lingering vacuum that haunts your every breath. But eventually, it will get you healed.

You will be stronger than you could ever imagine. You will know who you are truly meant to be. And in the end, you will be grateful it happened.

This journey is personal, but it's also remarkably universal. Whether it is a whirlwind romance, a scheming coworker, an abusive relative, or a life-threatening affair, a relationship with a narcissist is always the same. Your mind is left spinning. You feel useless and lost. You become numb to the essential things that once made you happy.

I cannot repair a toxic relationship (because toxic people cannot change), but I can give you a new place to start. And I can promise that you will be happy once again. You will eventually learn to trust your intuition. You will walk around this world with the knowledge of a survivor and the gentle marvel of a dreamer.

Initially, you'll need to forget everything you believed you understood about people. Understanding psychopathy needs releasing your fundamental emotional impulses. Remember, these are people who abuse forgiveness. They thrive on your need for closure. They manipulate empathy and exploit sympathy.

Since the dawn of time, psychopaths have waged mental warfare on others-- humiliating and shaming kind, unsuspecting victims-- people who never asked for it; people who aren't even aware of the war until it's over.

But this is about to change.

Say goodbye to love triangles, cryptic letters, insecurity, and produced stress and anxiety. You will never again find yourself desperately awaiting a text from the person you love or censor your spirit for fear of losing the "best" relationship. You will not be told to stop overanalyzing something that urgently needs analysis. You are no longer a pawn in the mind games of a narcissist. You are free.

And now it's time for your experience.

Your energy is minimal - that's a fundamental reality you have to accept. Just like a vehicle operating on gas, or a battery that's gradually drained power with each use, you too can run out of energy. What sets you apart from these inanimate power sources is that you have an option. You can choose where to spend your energy resources, and you can choose to prevent the vampires that sap you of vitality.

The unfortunate thing is that many of us don't know where or who these energy vampires may be. We end up basking in their existence, spending all our time with them, and losing our energy as a result of their toxic personalities.

Another issue is that many of us do not know why we need to avoid these kinds of people. What's so bad about having them hanging around? The important thing about your energy is that it gives you the power to go through your everyday life-- the less energy you have, the more difficult it is to manage all the things you have to do.

Hanging around a narcissistic relationship is an energy killer that can make you feel unhappy and exhausted and may make it challenging to find the determination to go through daily life. But there is more to them than that.

When a narcissist takes your positive energy, they replace it with negative energy. So aside from making you feel exhausted and unmotivated, they can also plant seeds of anger, hate, unhappiness, bitterness, and other unfriendly feelings that can have a substantial effect on your outlook and the way you relate to other significant people in your life.

Soon enough, you may be an energy vampire-- bringing a cloud of destruction, sadness, and anger to the lives of others around you. Which isn't something any of us should ever wish to be.

Narcissists are all around us, and some of them might be less obvious than others. Taking the form of a member of the family, friends, and trusted colleagues, these people can effectively conceal their real way and fool you into keeping them in your life so that they can exercise their power over your feelings.

If you can determine how to spot them in your life, you can cut them out, shut the door, and reduce your communications with them so that you will not have to suffer their toxicity.

Now, you might be asking, how can you tell where these narcissists are? What do they look like, and how do they act? If they're lovers, friends, or members of the family, how do you cut them out without making them feel unwanted or disrespected? And lastly, how can you protect yourself from allowing new ones to enter your life?

In this book, we're discussing anything and everything you need to learn about narcissistic characters and how these energy vampires can negatively affect all aspects of your life. We're also giving you all the strategies and tips you can use to protect yourself from their damaging practices.

CHAPTER ONE

Who Is A Narcissist

Let's start with a practical meaning of narcissism. Narcissists are people who feel that they are unique or special and therefore deserve to be treated as special by others. They often have grandiose and big-headed mindsets in their interactions with others and expect others to see their distinct skills and abilities.

Narcissists are generally frustrated unless they are getting tributes from those around them. They tend to lack empathy and have a limited capacity to love. Narcissists often have fantasies of unlimited power, luster, or wealth. They tend to make use of others to their ends and be distrustful of others.

In looking at this definition, you can see why it is complicated to deal with, be in a relationship with, or work with somebody who has a narcissistic personality condition or has deeply - rooted narcissistic characteristics.

Narcissists are characterized by a pervasive pattern of grandiosity (either in fantasy or in behavior), a constant need for appreciation, and an absence of compassion. Narcissism must be present by their early adult years and emerge in several contexts.

Five of the following nine criteria should be met for a diagnosis of narcissistic character condition:

- A grandiose sense of self-importance
- A fixation with fantasies of endless success, power, radiance, beauty, or perfect love
- A belief that she or he is special and unique and can only be comprehended by, or ought to associate with, other special or high-status people or institutions
- A need for extreme adoration
- A sense of privilege
- Interpersonally exploitive behavior
- A lack of compassion
- Jealousy of others or a belief that others are envious of him or her

- A presentation of arrogant and conceited habits or behaviors.

What Is a Psychopath Compared to a Narcissist?

According to the Society for the Scientific Study of Psychopathy, narcissism is an interpersonal sign of psychopathy. Symptoms of narcissism like grandiosity, exploitive habits, and an absence of sympathy are typical in psychopaths.

A psychopath could, and likely would quickly fit the medical diagnosis for narcissistic character condition as well; for that reason, psychopaths are narcissists.

Are Narcissists Psychopaths?

Just because an individual fits the criteria for narcissistic character condition does not mean that he or she is also a psychopath. To be considered a psychopath, many other demented signs such as an absence of attachment to others, shallow charm, dishonesty, manipulativeness, and negligent risk-taking come into play. Psychopathic narcissists exist, but they are not the standard.

How to Deal With Narcissists

A prevailing pattern of grandiosity, need for affection, lack of empathy, as indicated by a minimum of five of the following:

1. a grand sense of self-importance.

2. is preoccupied with fantasies of endless success, power, luster, charm, or perfect love.

3. thinks that she or he is "special" and can just be comprehended by, or need to connect with, other unique or high-status people (or institutions).

4. needs excessive adoration.

5. has a sense of privilege, i.e., unreasonable expectations of especially favorable treatment or automated compliance with his/her expectations.

6. is interpersonally exploitative, i.e., takes benefit of others to achieve his/her ends.

7. lacks compassion and hesitates to acknowledge or determine with the feelings and needs of others.

8. is frequently envious of others or believes that others are envious of him or her.

9. programs big-headed, haughty behaviors, or attitudes.

Have you ever met somebody with some of these qualities? You were likely dealing with somebody who was at least slightly narcissistic. I think what defines a narcissistic personality is someone who thinks they indeed are "the bee's knees." They believe they are much better than everybody else, should have special treatment, and seem to reside in their little world. In common parlance: SELFISH. There's usually an 'entitlement' thing going on, where he/she acts like a king or a queen and expects people to drop everything to 'serve' him/her.

Many females have the experience of being raised by parents like this and being in friendships and intimate relationships with such people. They come to a therapy feeling 'insane' because they are upset with such people, but do not think they ought to be because the narcissistic person has encouraged them .

Narcissists are some of the most crazy-making and discouraging people to deal with in deep space. I hope that you have no idea what I have just spoken about because you've never experienced it, but I bet you do know from personal experience. Narcissism abounds in this crazy world of ours.

To secure yourself from people like this, use the requirements for narcissism mentioned at the start of this book to identify whether someone in your life may be narcissistic. Do everything you have to do to secure yourself from being a victim of this person and their insanity. There are many excellent books and sites out there, which will help you in this vein. I recommend research on the internet or your local library's brochure. Read as much as you can. Educate yourself. Take the actions needed to protect yourself and your children (if they are affected). It might be practical to see a credible psychotherapist as they will have the ability to give you handy tools to learn self-care in the face of narcissistic characters. In some cases, this means escaping these people all together, and sometimes you can have milder but indirect contact. The most important thing to keep in mind in dealing with these people is that it is they who have the issue, not you.

Living or working with somebody who is narcissistic can be very frustrating and sometimes extremely traumatic. If you're having an affair with a narcissist, you may see yourself asking, "When will it ever have to do with me?" You might ultimately come to realize that you will never be a priority in the life of your self-absorbed other. This is a hard realization to come to, but what keeps people locked into their narcissistic other is the hope that someday the individual will snap out of it or happen to love others. Isn't that what we all want: to feel a connection with others, to love and be loved? For narcissists, in some way, this need for connection and love gets obscured.

From Self-Loathing to Healthy Self-Love to Narcissism

In talking about narcissism, it is practical to think of an individual's feelings about himself as being on a continuum. At one end of the continuum is self-loathing or self-hatred. We all know people like this. They are very self-critical, and if you compliment them, they will create a way to downplay it. This character trait is the opposite of narcissism. In the middle of the continuum is healthy self-love. This can best be referred to as happening when people value themselves, they look after themselves, and they can stick up for themselves. A person who accepts healthy self-love can love others because she is confident in herself and, for that reason, can express love without fear of being injured or rejected. People who epitomize healthy self-love are most likely to engage in charitable habits.

Narcissism falls at the other end of the continuum. It is defined by people who are so narcissistic and caught up in their plan that they can't see other people or their needs. As with the legendary Narcissus, they are caught up in their reflection and image. Therefore, they are incapable of caring for others and can just love themselves.

CHAPTER TWO

Different Level and Types of Narcissism

Narcissism exists in people in varying degrees. With the dawn of social media, the majority of us display specific narcissistic characteristics to some extent. For instance, you might consider yourself more attractive than so-and-so, as evidenced by the variety of likes your selfies get online compared to that person.

For us, nevertheless, this kind of narcissism is harmless because it does not honestly do anything to tear other people down or destroy relationships. The narcissistic thoughts are just ever kept inside because we know the kind of damage they would create if we let them out.

This ability to manage the way we think about others and filter what we allow to come through is a sign of empathy-- we don't want to hurt so-and-so, so we keep our mouths shut and keep our ideas hush-hush.

Good narcissism exists in most of us and takes the kind of minor self- principles that put us above others. This is the most common symptom and usually doesn't vocalize or open to anyone around us. These thoughts merely make us feel much better about ourselves, and that's it. They're not used against other people, and they're not harmful the way deadly narcissists do.

Reasonably narcissistic people might deal with some damage to others around them, although to a lesser level than severe narcissists. These people might have some insight about their narcissistic propensities, perhaps after knowing that one or both of their parents were narcissists themselves.

They might act out and put pressure on others, but then recant what they say later when they feel far more in tune with their feelings. They may struggle to control themselves but still can recognize when they've overdone it.

Sometimes, their partners might find them difficult at best. But at the end of the day, they're ready to come to a compromise and may even apologize for their behavior, not to manipulate others, but because they see the error of their actions and want to make it right. In any case, these narcissists have the best opportunity of recovering from their character and might even have the ability to do it without the need for treatment or therapy.

Extreme narcissists are the worst of their kind. Frequently called deadly narcissists, these people will abuse anyone and everybody that subjects themselves to the narcissist's control. They handle to get a few people to submit to their desires, which feeds their narcissistic needs because they can be quite lovely and charismatic.

These people need a constant 'narcissistic supply' or a group of people that they exploit to feed their ego. This might include their family and friends. If anything, these narcissists are what you may call 'energy vampires' because of their character, which can sap anybody of positivity and determination.

Distancing yourself from severe narcissists can help spare you from their assault and keep you feeling healthy and mentally well-balanced.

In terms of the types of narcissists, there are many. These often don't exist separately, particularly in extreme narcissists who showcase any of these qualities in a mix with one another:

Know-It-All - Aside from feeling like they're always right and fault-free, this kind of narcissist thinks they're entitled to a view in any given scenario. It doesn't matter if the person they're talking with is an old friend, a family member of the authority, a manager, or an associate they just met, these narcissists will exercise their 'right' to give an opinion even when it's unsolicited.

They can be nasty to be around, especially if you weren't always trying to find advice on particular topics. What makes it worse is that if you refuse their commentary, they'll brand you dumb for thinking otherwise. Usually, these narcissists don't honestly want to listen to a conversation.

So even if you're talking right in front of them, they're not likely to be listening. Instead, they're probably thinking of what they want to say next and might even cut your speech short to get to talk finally.

-Grandiose - They see themselves as the best, and they're not afraid to express that. Grand narcissists think themselves to be best in all ways and promote their supremacy, typically making others around them either feel a strong sense of adoration or a strong dislike for their boastful behavior.

They'll frequently speak about their achievements, their assets, and all the other 'amazing' things that they have experienced. Even in a setting when the focus is on specific people, they will discover a way to make aspects of themselves. A grandiose narcissist may find it suitable to propose to his sweetheart in the middle of a friend's wedding event reception.

While narcissists are generally successful people because of their unrelenting drive to have something to show for, you might discover that some grandiose narcissists inflate their possessions to drive more attention. Sometimes, there might even be a disparity between what they say and who they are. A lady who made millions in her prime who goes through monetary confusion twenty years later on might still be talking about her millions even if they're long gone.

-Bully - The narcissistic bully rears its awful head typically when it feels threatened by someone around them. For instance, you may find your co-worker flexing particular techniques to make your work experience less than satisfying. They might discuss you to other co-workers, tell them to stay away from you, and may even intentionally do things to make the daily grind a hassle.

What this narcissist is awaiting is for you to snap. They desire to provoke you so they can have the phase and show everybody how they can ' win' against anybody, and how nobody must have the gall to take them on because they usually are 'better' and 'smarter.' You may discover yourself in a scrape once you are provoked, and you do give in.

-Vindictive - The vindictive narcissist is the worst kind of severe narcissist. When you engage in an argument with a narcissist and overtly display your dislike for their behavior, this takes place. At this point, the narcissist has tossed all care and factor to the wind and enacts several tactics to make your life an ordeal.

They'll do anything to hurt you, and they'll commemorate your defeat. Frequently, they'll turn people against you so that you have no one in your corner when things get heated. They'll dismantle your reputation and make you feel unloved and unwanted. When it comes to a narcissistic member of the family, they may separate you completely.

Narcissistic vs. narcissistic Personality Disorder

To some extent, some of us manifest narcissistic qualities. Especially with the dawn of social media, it's easy to fall into the trap of comparing ourselves to others and attempting to boost our truth to seem more astounding than the lives we genuinely lead.

It's crucial to comprehend that nevertheless, there is a fine line that separates typical narcissistic behavior from full-blown Narcissistic Personality Disorder (NPD). The two are different in that NPD is an identified mental condition, while narcissism explains a group of actions that aren't always a sign of psychological distress.

An individual with NPD will be caught between two worlds. They feel superior to others. And second, they likely have a fragile sense of self- worth. So, while they will generally parade around revealing their successes and accomplishments and how these things make them better than a lot of other people, it's also possible that they struggle with serious self-esteem issues.

When faced with any kind of criticism, they shut down, explode into fits of anger, or perhaps go through episodes of depression. People with NPD struggle to engage typically with their friends and family members. They will tend to isolate themselves instead, saying they're 'too great' for others around them while safeguarding themselves from potential vulnerability.

On the other hand, narcissistic people hunger for admiration and approval. In our society, these people may just seem like they're obnoxious and arrogant, because they lack the empathy it takes to understand how they make other people feel. They aim for achievement, and they do not care who they step on along the way.

These people also have a propensity for making others feel secondary or merely less capable. They aren't reluctant to put others down, specifically if it helps to highlight their achievements. So, they'll typically talk about how they're the best at their vocation, and how others in the same field aren't as good as they are.

Another thing that sets narcissists apart from people with NPD is the truth that they don't usually experience vulnerable egos. They rain on other people's parade because they feel that their superiority provides the right to. This is opposed to people with NPD who inflate their self-worth to draw attention far from their flaws and avoid criticism.

In history, there have been many prominent political and public figures with narcissistic qualities that today personify evil as we understand it. Adolf Hitler, Pol Pot, and Josef Stalin were all discovered to demonstrate some narcissistic attributes and tendencies, which is how they got power in the first place.

Essentially, a Narcissistic Personality Disorder is a mental health condition. These people experience a condition that affects their social and occupational efficiency. Narcissists, on the other hand, are just about themselves and their image, particularly when taken against to others around them.

These people hunger for adoration, cash, status, and power, and will do everything to obtain that, even if it means stepping on people they call family and friends.

Finally, it's also essential for you to comprehend that people with narcissistic propensities do not require you to sympathize with them. One of the causes that it's so easy for some people to come down with an energy vampire is because they feel that they should nurture and nurse that person's 'broken' sense of self-worth.

Unlike individuals with NPD, people who show narcissistic habits aren't lacking self-esteem. They have enough to walk around. So instead of trying to understand and forgive them, tread gently. You stand to lose rather a lot by trying to fix someone who may not think there's anything wrong.

Personality Disorder vs. Personality Traits.

A person can exhibit some narcissistic traits but not necessarily manifest the full-blown personality disorder. One of the essential differences here is that people with NPD typically display narcissistic characteristics or attributes that are both maladaptive and prevalent.

Is the person in your life a narcissist?

You can start to address this problem by taking a record of his or her narcissistic traits.

Exercise: Place a checkmark beside any of the following narcissistic characteristics that would apply to the person you know. **You May Be Dealing with a Narcissist If;**

- It's always about him or her, not about you.
- His or her desires or needs always come before yours.
- She or he is proficient at making you feel inferior.
- You often feel exploited or used by him or her.
- She or he needs your admiration and consistent attention.
- He or she often acts in an arrogant, hoity-toity manner.

- He or she lacks compassion and has difficulty showing caring feelings.
- He or she is good at charming people or selling people on his or her ideas.
- He or she typically wants to be in a position of power or have control over others.
- She or he feels that the rules do not apply in his/her case.
- She or he is thoughtful with fantasies of wealth and popularity.
- He or she is seen as a blowhard by good friends or loved ones.

Possibilities are if you examined three or more of the above traits, you might be dealing with somebody with narcissistic personality qualities or narcissistic personality disorder.

It is just to get sucked in by a narcissist's wit, charm, or charisma. He will often have rather a flair for winning people over or offering them on his ideas. It is no surprise, then, that narcissists are drawn in to positions of power or in the affair which they have the upper hand, yet they want to be around others whom they view as complementing their beauty. Keep in mind, nevertheless, that in any relationship, narcissists are only out for themselves or what they believe they can get out of the relationship, not what they can give to the relationship.

Subtypes or Variations of Narcissistic Personality Disorder.

Not all narcissists are the same. Psychologist Theodore Millon (1996) explained the following subtypes of people with NPD:

- the unprincipled narcissist,
- the amorous narcissist,
- the countervailing narcissist,
- and the elitist narcissist.

As you check out these subtypes, see if any look comparable to the person you have issues with. Note that both males and females can fall into any of these categories, and the narcissist in your life may display characteristics of more than one subtype.

- **The Unprincipled Narcissist.**

What identifies unprincipled narcissists is that they appear to be devoid of a conscience or sense of right and wrong. They are often careless with the well-being of others and are amoral, deceitful, and deceptive in their negotiations with others. They exhibit a big-headed sense of self-respect and grandiosity. They are driven by a need to outsmart others, which shows that they are smarter than their victim. It's not rare to find this type of narcissist in prisons, and drug rehabilitation centers, although lots of unprincipled narcissists go through life without running afoul of the law.

- **The Amorous Narcissist.**

Amorous narcissists have a sexual or seductive orientation. They build and determine their self-respect around sexual conquests. They typically run through a string of unhealthy relationships, casting aside the individual they have simply seduced just to search for their next win. Amorous narcissists are frequently known for being heartbreakers, in addition to committing some rather outrageous acts, such as tricking their sexual partners out of vast amounts of money, pathological lying, and other kinds of deceptive behavior. The amorous narcissist is the Don Juan charisma who makes up for much more profound feelings of insufficiency by seducing others and taking them for all they're worth. Each sexual conquest improves the amorous narcissist's sense of self-respect and overinflated self-image.

- **The Compensatory Narcissist.**

The countervailing narcissist is driven by a need to compensate for previous injures or youth psychological wounds by developing an illusion of supremacy. Compensatory narcissists live in a fictional world of their development in which they "pursue the leading role in a fictional and false theater" (Millon 1996, 411) rather than living their own lives.

They are driven to improve their self- esteem through what are frequently thought of accomplishments. To accomplish this goal of eminence, compensatory narcissists need an audience of others who will buy into their deception. In reality, countervailing narcissists are extraordinarily delicate or typically hypervigilant to how others react to or view them, frequently seeing or thoroughly listening for any signs of criticism or contempt.

- **The Elitist Narcissist.**

In some ways similar to countervailing narcissists, elitist narcissists are frequently obsessed with their inflated self-image. They often develop a false sense of self that bears little similarity to their real person. Yet, they manage to convince themselves (and typically those around them) of their unique skills and abilities. They feel empowered and entitled to unique treatment because of whatever status or pseudo-achievements they might have achieved. Elitist narcissists often turn relationships into competitions or contests, whether they are work relationships, friendships, and even love relationships. Here the objective is winning, no matter what the methods or cost, to prove to others (and themselves) their unparalleled superiority. Elitist narcissists are typically social climbers, and they downplay stepping on or over anyone in their mission for popularity and status. They are very skilled at marketing themselves and will not shrink from any chance to do so. They see no reason to listen to others or follow instructions because elitist narcissists hold themselves in such high esteem.

Other Narcissistic Subtypes are:

In dealing with people, we see a fair bit of privilege and narcissistic behavior, and we've established our list of more common subtypes that appear to fit with the times. As you check out the subtypes, which follow, do any look similar to the narcissist in your life?

The trust fund baby: Rather similar to Theodore Millon's elitist narcissist (1996), trust fund babies are narcissists who grew up with the proverbial silver spoon in their mouth and have no hesitancy about letting others know of their pedigree, their financial worth, what unique prep school they went to, and so on. What's often extremely fascinating about these narcissists is that they matured feeling special and therefore entitled. As a result, they usually have little ability for empathy and limited time or interest in anybody whom they perceive to be of lower social status.

When it comes to the individual troubles of others, as Marie Antoinette put it, "Let them eat cake!" Naturally, not everyone born to wealth and privilege becomes a narcissist; some do exceptionally philanthropic work and aspire to occupations in which they do greats on behalf of others.

-**The profession-bound narcissist**: There are narcissists whose whole identity is tied up in who they are as professionals. Whether they are medical professionals, lawyers, judges, monetary specialists, academics, actors, or musicians, their egos are so enormous that they need a tractor-trailer to transport them around. These are people who like to flaunt their power and, in doing so, are typically abusive to anyone who crosses their course or gets in their way. You'll see these peoples driving around in the latest sports cars with vanity license plates as if announcing to the world what they do for a living. Consider it this way: when somebody is genuinely at the top of his field, does he truly have to flaunt it?

-**The child prodigy narcissist**: Some people believe they are unique and special because they grew up with a lot of adults, always advising them that they were. From the star athlete to the talented musician to the most talented trainee, they got more than their share of the magnificence and distinctions while maturing. This early popularity seems to enter their heads, as they too start to feel that they are larger than life. We hear many stories of child stars and prodigies who end up having miserable adult lives that are ruined by drug or alcohol addiction and psychological chaos. Just being typical or being a face in the crowd is not okay for these narcissists, who require to be recognized and the center of attention wherever they go. It's no surprise that former child prodigies often cannot stand the fact that they no longer have a unique status. We typically see them in the university setting: having come through talented and gifted programs in grade school and high school, these former kid prodigies often conclude that their skills will bring them through college-level courses without having to put in the work to get an A. Since they're entitled to it, they often feel they ought to be given an A.

-The closet narcissist: Probably the hardest to discern, closet narcissists frequently appear on the surface area to be just like everybody else. It's not until you get to know them or you scratch below the surface that you begin to see their real selves. When this happens, you begin to see their haughtiness, expectation, and arrogance to be treated as unique, or their need to put in power over others. What makes these narcissists hard to define is that they typically look for out occupations or positions in which you ordinarily would not expect to find narcissists, such as in human services, in teaching, and even amongst the clergy. What is evident after some time is that they are not about helping others but about self-glorification. They are not about assisting those whom they are expected to serve but about building their egos up (at others' cost).

-The know-it-all narcissist: This subtype looks like the profession-bound narcissist, but you may find this kind of narcissist in nearly any walk of life. Typically these know-it-alls lack an inclusive education, but they go through life browbeating others into coming around to their mindset. They usually have incredible viewpoints about almost whatever, and they feel they have been put on this earth to offer up their little pearls of wisdom on anything unsuspecting victim happens to give them an ear. Know-it-alls can be expected to be best about whatever-- keep in mind the cardinal guideline "Don't confuse them with the realities," since their minds are made up, and they will be unrelenting until they have changed your mind also. Sometimes it's best simply to let them rant and rave and to go on your merry way. If you are a captive audience, hopefully, your perseverance will hold up.

The addicted narcissist: One of the regrettable by-products of dependency (whether it be to drugs, alcohol, betting, shopping, or sex) is that addicts are incapable of caring for others. One sure sign of dependency is that an addict will consistently put a drug of choice over loved ones. It goes with the area, which is why addicts will downplay stealing from their families, lying, or conning them. This kind of behavior can be seen as a type of narcissism, albeit drug-induced but a narcissistic process nevertheless.

One of the incredible changes that happen when someone truly accepts healing (and begins to build a structured, constant recovery program) is that you start to see a transformation from a narcissistic or egocentric way of life to one in which the now recovering individual can love others and get involved fully in caring relationships. Sadly, we had also seen circumstances where people claim to be recuperating but remain as self-indulgent as they were when they were actively addicted. Generally, this absence of change or development can be traced back to something lacking in the way they've worked their healing program.

CHAPTER THREE

Narcissism in Relationships

Being in a love relationship with a narcissist can be frustrating. Some compete that it is difficult, if not impossible, to be involved in a real love relationship with a narcissist because the narcissist is just in love with herself. Although you might sometimes wish for an equal partnership, it never appears to happen. Because narcissists don't wear signs saying "Beware: I am only capable of loving myself," it's widespread for people to find themselves in love with someone whose narcissistic characteristics do not appear until in the relationship.

Early on, it may be hard to tell. Narcissists are often quite charming and extremely competent at what is called impression management. Some are keenly experts about how to check out people and react appropriately. With time, nevertheless, narcissists start to reveal their real colors.

It's typical for people to be blind to their partner's narcissism, given the narcissist's capability to create a positive impression.

Partners of narcissists will typically discuss the narcissist's several admirable qualities, such as his self-confidence or her sense of humor or how great he is as a financial service provider. In the general scope of the relationship, partners of narcissists typically feel that something is missing. Although it may be difficult at first to know what that thing is, it generally becomes evident over time. Partners typically find themselves initially being angry or irritated in social circumstances when the narcissistic spouse or partner always guides the discussion toward his conquests or achievements; they discover that the narcissistic partner needs to be the focal point, no matter what the event.

The Narcissist as a Friend

Just like love relationships, extreme self-centeredness is an issue in friendships with narcissists. You may find that you are always there for your narcissistic friend, but somehow she is never there for you. Or you might find yourself continually doing what he wants and on his schedule, but somehow you never get around to doing things that you want to do or at your benefit. Being the best friend of a narcissist is not a simple task; however, in a relationship, you have a much better opportunity of limiting your contact. In a love relationship or a work setting, you may be a captive audience to the narcissist's exquisite game, which is often created to exploit you and to aggrandize the narcissist.

How Do Narcissists Get That Way?

With all the talk about the influences of genes and neurotransmitters on behavior, you may question if there is some hereditary link to narcissistic personality condition or some chemical imbalance that triggers it. Regrettably, although it's tempting to draw such a conclusion, it's likely that narcissists are not born that way but establish narcissistic qualities.

The two theories provided here are among the most popular and convincing. One of these theories is that people develop narcissistic traits in response to how they were parented. The other approach is that these qualities evolve out of deep-seated feelings of inferiority.

- **Parenting Style**

Many teenagers are narcissistic and undoubtedly self-indulgent. It seems to go with the territory of being a teen. Teens have an exceptional talent for seeing life through only their own eyes of teenage angst. This is among the reasons why teens can be so cruel and bullying to their parents or peers. However, a lot of people who endure teenage years can shed their egocentric views and begin to establish a sense of empathy for others, specifically as they start to develop the capacity to look at things from different perspectives.

You might well ask whether this means she will grow up to become a narcissist if you have a teenage child who is very self-indulgent. The response is probably not. One reason that teens are never detected with character disorders is that their characters are still developing. As a parent, you can motivate your egocentric teen to put herself in the other person's shoes or to look at things from other people's points of view. This may help her establish empathy. Some teenagers are naturall empathic, and seeing things from another's point of view comes to them more easily. For others, compassion takes some time to develop, specifically if they've been accustomed to having things go their method or they've received some attention or honors.

It appears that those who go on to become full-fledged narcissists, nevertheless, might have experienced a parenting design that was either overindulgent and indulging or neglectful and rejecting. Freud (1914) was among the early theorists to describe this kind of parenting style. Some narcissistic personalities were parented in such a way to convey that they were the center of the universe. This holds of "phase moms" and "coach fathers" who teach their kids that the world must and does revolve around them. This might also take place in child-centered families in which the marital bond is rather weak or nonexistent; it is much easier for these couples to focus their lives around their kid.

In the opposite situation, where moms and dads are neglectful, rejecting, or often fickle or irregular, children learn that they cannot depend on their parents for nurturance or love. These children give up relying on that their parents will love them and turn to the only person they feel they can depend on themselves. This shift towards self-love is viewed as an effort at self- conservation.

- **Compensating for Feelings of Inferiority**

Another theory that helps to explain why some people become narcissists and others don't is found in the philosophy of settlement (Reich 1960). This theory is that narcissism is rooted in feelings of inability; to conquer these feelings, the narcissist embraces a pattern of behavior in which he overcompensates by overachieving. Akhtar and Thomson (1982) discuss that although people with NPD appear grandiose, sexy, and exploitative, they are doubt-ridden, chronically bored, jealous of others' accomplishments, and unable to love. Their overcompensation is typically played out in such areas as occupational endeavors, financial success, or having the most attractive mate. We've all seen people who overcompensate by buying the expensive cars, the largest or fastest boats, or the most elegant penthouse condominium. It is as if they were saying, "Look at me; see how successful I am." The old joke "the bigger the cars, the smaller the penis" may not be that far from the truth. It might be a sensation of smallness, or inability, which causes some narcissists to behave the way they do.

It may seem contradictory that those who harbor feelings of inferiority would wish to accentuate themselves. Still, the theory is that in doing so, they are trying to get the adoration of other people. Narcissists may see themselves as adorable based on their ability to get others to love them, and they, therefore, feel obliged to draw attention to themselves so that others will see how adorable and admirable they are.

Are You Dealing with a Narcissist?

You may be asking the question "Is the person in my life truly a narcissist?" This session will assist you in answering that question more definitively by taking a more detailed look at the other person's behaviors and their impact on you.

This part will give you a fresh understanding of your history with this person, allowing you to translate problematic interactions in a new way. You must discover this not only informing but likewise beneficial as you begin to build much better-coping strategies.

Having the ability to identify your difficulties with the other person accurately is the beginning of real service. In the past, it may have appeared that you were going from one knotted and confusing interaction to another, leaving you hurt and bewildered. Now you will have the ability to recognize the other person's strategies so clearly that they will stand apart like flashing neon signs pointing the way toward a far more effective response from you.

The Narcissist Change the Way You Think, Feel, and Act

Narcissists will make you think differently, feel differently, and act in a different way than anyone else. Narcissists affect you in a much more profound and more pervasive way than other "difficult" people. There are people whom you just might not like for one reason or another, but, for the many parts, when you deal with them, you are entirely yourself. When you are with somebody who has narcissistic characteristics, but, it's like you develop another character, one that you do not like too much. Whereas formerly you might have been friendly and outbound, around the narcissist, you feel reserved and shy. Usually, when you are around others, you think that your viewpoints are intelligent and well-considered. Still, when you're involved in a conversation with a narcissist, you feel that what you have to say is stupid and irrelevant. If you are generally well-spoken, you will stammer. You will be a bungler around the narcissist if you are good at your job. Because you cannot be yourself when you are around this person, you are merely not yourself and most likely are upset with yourself.

Some psychologists refer to this process as projective recognition. A simple method to explain this rather complicated behavioral interaction is that the narcissist somehow makes you believe a role that will meet her needs. For example, if a narcissist needs to have a dispute or argue with someone, you will find yourself unexpectedly wishing to argue and debate. This will be true even if you are typically not the kind of person who likes to argue. If a narcissist needs to seduce others, you might find yourself sexually attracted to him, even if you are not looking for a sexual partner. We know that sounds odd, but it's true. It nearly looks like a magic spell has been cast on you that utterly change you.

Another way to tell you are involved with a narcissist is that the other person appears to occupy all your thoughts all of the time. This can be exceptionally odd. You just can't help it. You see yourself focused on the other person. A different way of putting this is that the narcissist lives in your brain rent complimentary. You find yourself wishing to think about other things, but you can't. Not only will you continuously think about the narcissist, but you will find this person partaking in your conversations in the strangest ways. You will be speaking about the new car you are considering purchasing one minute, and the next minute you'll be talking about your narcissistic brother who never does his share around the holidays.

How Does Your Attitude Change Around the Narcissist?

Place a checkmark next to the following ways that you have or acted in response to this person that appear different from the way you would generally operate. With this person, you do the following:

-avoid confrontations

-avoid crucial conversations that may result in you being personally assaulted or put down subjugate your requirements

-pull more than your weight run after the person to bring him or her back into the relationship always

- assure the other person on how great he or she is used to alcohol or drugs to handle this relationship

-have distressing dreams about the other person

-lose sleep over this person

-are reduced to tears on more than one party

-spend a lot of time thinking of the relationship

-abide by the other person's unreasonable demands even when you are highly inconvenienced or sick

-take medications to manage this relationship

-look for expert help

-sacrifice time in other relationships or activities

Exercises: How Does Your Thinking Change in Reaction to the Narcissist?

Place a checkmark next to any of the following ideas that you have had in reaction to the narcissistic person:

-He or she is humiliating you on purpose.

-You are just not that important.

-You are stuck in this relationship.

-You are incredibly foolish for being in this relationship.

-You should be faithful and devoted and not leave this relationship.

-This person never plays by the rules.

-He or she will exploit you for sure if you do not keep your guard up all the time.

-This relationship is the worst thing that might ever happen to you.

-You are so dumb for letting this person get to you.

-You simply can't take on him or her.

-You can never change the circumstance.

-This person will entirely control you if you allow him or her.

Because of your defects, the reason that this relationship doesn't go your way is;

-In some way, you did something to deserve this.

-As long as the other individual is around, you will never get what you want.

-The circumstance will never end; it will continuously be the same.

-At times, this person wants to disgrace you.

-This person will use you, no matter what you do.

-You can never please his/her.

-Things would be better if only you might change somehow and become more like this person wants you to be.

-You are attracted to this relationship like a moth to a flame.

-Being around this individual in some way makes you more vital.

-You will never get through to this person; you can never get your point in.

-This person is so skilled or talented that you need to support him or her in these ventures.

-This person could not care less about your feelings.

-List some other thoughts you have had in response to this person:

Examine your reactions to these exercises carefully. Did you mark off a number of the items? What do you think? Remember, narcissists, change the way you believe, feel, and act. Do you think that your ideas, feelings, and habits with this person are incredibly different from those you have with other significant people in your life? Do you discover that you are not yourself when communicating with this person? If so, you are probably dealing with a narcissist.

The Narcissist Takes Advantage of You

In addition to making you feel, behave, and think in particular ways, which are different from how you are with others, the narcissist will probably have done things to you that others have not. Narcissists can be exploitative, crossing over typically accepted borders to make the most of those around them.

The narcissist greedy sense of privilege makes it easy for him to make use of those around him; after all, he is such an exceptional person; he deserves what he takes. They should have given it to him in the first place.

Exercise: Is the Person in Your Life Exploitative?

Each of the following statements explains how a narcissist may be exploitative. Complete the blanks using a scale of 1 to 5:

1. She or he borrowed or takes money without paying it back.

2. This person takes credit for something that he or she did not do

3. He or she desires exceptional sexual favors.

4. He or she takes things without asking first.

5. This individual ruins or ruins the items that he or she never offers to repair or change.

6. He or she physically abuses you or others.

7. She or he makes sexual advances towards somebody you had a romantic interest in.

8. This person spreads out reports about you or misrepresents you in some way so that he or she will look great.

9. This person insists that you take part in among his or her self-serving programs.

10. He or she insists that you do something unpleasant or highly troublesome.

11. She or he insults belittles or hurts those you are close to, generally without apology.

12. She or he breaks rules that to everyone else uses.

13. This person asks one of your acquaintances to do something bothersome or undesirable even though she or he barely knows that person.

14. This person lies to you for his or her gain.

15. She or he makes you look silly or foolish in the business of others (such as making you the butt of a joke or informing an embarrassing story about you).

Now accumulate the score. A rating of over 55 recommends that the individual in your life is exploitative.

Now list some particular instances in which this person has tried to exploit you or used you. Examples may be "Even though we have separated, he wants me to come over when he is sick to clean his wounds and get his medications.

Your examples:

Time for some self-reflection. Does the fact that the person in your life exploits you and others because she or he feels entitled to do so make you see things a little differently? What has changed? How will having this knowledge enable you to act differently when this person gets help from you? If you can't think of anything right now, don't stress. This subject will be thoroughly covered in later chapters.

The Narcissist Engages in Splitting Behaviors

Psychologists use the term splitting to describe the procedure of seeing the world in black-and-white terms with no gradations of gray. Splitting is a propensity to misestimate people, events, concepts, products, activities, and any other thing you could call, just to quickly cheapen these things after discovering any kind of defect in them. People who do this see others in their lives as either terrific or terrible, handy or ineffective, hot or repulsive, winners or losers. There is no happy medium for them. If the narcissist in your life has this tendency, you are either a moron or a genius, somebody she can either worship or walk all over.

It is essential to note here that the constant usage of splitting as a defense system is generally the sign of a severe disorder. It is regularly seen with a borderline personality disorder, which is a disorder related to narcissism. While the conversation of this Disorder is beyond the scope of this book, it's enough to say that people with borderline personality disorder are best understood for being involved in tempestuous and astoundingly disrupted relationships, which remain in big part sustained by the process of splitting. The idea of splitting applies to all types of narcissistic relationship problems, and comprehending how it works with narcissism is crucial to disarming a narcissist and disengaging from his toxic plans.

One of the keys to understanding narcissism in the person you know is to admit that the narcissist takes part in splitting not only with others but also with himself. This will help you to get a handle on the other person's seemingly inconsistent moods and habits, which may appear to change on a dime. One narcissistic salesperson felt that to be qualified, he would need to sell a million dollars' worth of product in three months. He would feel on top of the world if he succeeded in this. He would date the most attractive women in town and complete in his favorite sport, which was racing motorboats. He would work out at the health club, refining his body to Olympian proportions while dressing just in the most beautiful clothing. If he sold even a hundred dollars less than his million-dollar goal, nevertheless, he would go into a duration of self-loathing, where he would just lie around all the time, neglecting his hobbies and his social life and sensation he was an ugly, despicable failure. It was just throughout this time that he would seek out a therapist to restore his self-esteem.

It may be some small consolation to know that what the narcissist does to others he also does to himself. You may wonder, where does splitting stem? Many psychologists think that splitting is an early form of information processing. Vitally young children know the world only in regards to white and black; significant variations and subtle gradations are far too complicated for their young minds to comprehend, and seeing them needs additional brain advancement. It is crucial to know here that everyone has tendencies to split under certain conditions. For example, we tend to misestimate food when we are extremely hungry; food that would generally disgust us may suddenly look good. When we are in a rush to get to our works, and the highways are bumper-to-bumper, everybody seems like an idiot, and it's tough to find any use for other people whatsoever.

Splitting is among the many mental defense systems people use when they feel threatened in some method. Narcissistic people can seem to be instead stuck in this information-processing mode. With the narcissist, splitting can be extreme. Possibly this is because narcissists are continuously living in a veiled but nonstop state of desperation, with all of their alarm systems locked to red-alert status, alerting them that their self-esteem is in critical jeopardy.

The Narcissistic Wound

Surprisingly, despite their bluster and big-headed personalities, narcissists can be enormously sensitive to criticisms and personal failures.

That proud and grand exterior typically hides a scared and embarrassed kid who is scared that his insufficiencies will be exposed? This revelation can be stunning to practically anyone involved with a narcissist: "Are you playing me? That self-infatuated, egotistical, and overconfident jerk of a boyfriend of mine who hits on anything with a skirt? Embarrassed as a little child?" It is all too real. It makes sense if you think about it.

So, how did that embarrassed kid mature to be this self-centered, egotistical maniac? Karen Horney (1991) provides a prominent explanation of this development. As a young kid, the narcissist has, like all of us, her unique personality filled with her matchless feelings, needs, and understandings. This is what Horney calls the real self; it is the narcissist's true identity. Problems develop, nevertheless, when a crucial person in the kid's life-- usually a mom and dad-- does not validate (or even like or approve of) all or part of the kid's character and therefore is decreasing. Disapproval may take the kind of destructive criticisms, withdrawals of love, shaming, and all other types of insensitive and harsh rejection. The kid's real self then becomes her disliked self; she merely hates herself for being, firstly, a failure in her parent's eyes and, then later, in her own eyes. She now cheapens and hates anything real in herself: she comes to define herself as weak, stupid, lacking in skill, afraid, blameworthy, and, in basic, disgraceful.

One way to look at the disliked self is that it is a gaping, bleeding injury that the narcissist is always trying to shield at all costs. It is a disgraceful and exceptionally uncomfortable wound indeed, and to have it exposed through the revealing of her imperfections would be an excruciating and devastating embarrassment that is just next to a slow and uncomfortable death. This narcissistic wound is intense and its never-ending defense is the last thing that drives the narcissist, like a shark, that must continue to swim just to breathe. A narcissistic high-school drama coach who was hypersensitive about his weight when reported this revealing dream was naked by a crowd, beaten until he bled all over, connected to a pole, and paraded through the streets as thousands of people lined up to jeer and humiliate him. That is a picture of the disliked self.

The narcissist's solution to this unbearable state of affairs is to develop another identity, one that Horney calls the perfect self and which is an effort to mask and make up for the despised person. In other words, the ideal self is the narcissist's marvelous option to his disliked self: Where he was once weak, he is now a hero-- no, a superhero-- undefeatable in all that he does. Where she was once unattractive, she is now captivating, sexy, and irresistible, the next supermodel replete with adoring fans and paparazzi. And where he was once without skill, he is now the world's foremost authority on, well, you call it. Discuss overcompensation. Now take all these things and inflate them to even bigger proportions-- that's the idealized self.

In the inmost parts of their minds, narcissists are acutely mindful from their scenarios that the idealized self is a huge lie: They discover out that the waitress that they were trying to impress by leaving big suggestions was truly giggling at their bloated pomposity behind their backs; the unique they believed to be the next best seller is still not completed; and they were not able to attain an erection the last 3 times they tried to consummate their newest seduction. They were turned down for the second time for a promotion, their formal friend in the world won't return their calls, and they still can't seem to lose that excess thirty pounds. Each one of these embarrassments resembles a jolting body punch of truth-- more salt put into the existing injuries of youth. They have been exposed! Now they hate themselves even more. Rather than acknowledge their drawbacks as just being human characteristics, narcissists will compensate with an even grander and more exceptional version of themselves. This technique will also soon fail, as it is even more unobtainable than the one before. The idealized self-image is an impossibly unattainable dream, which can only lead the narcissist into a series of embarrassing defeats. The procedure repeats itself over and over: trying to be a superman, only to stop working and suffer embarrassment, then disliking themselves and compensating once again by fashioning an even greater superman-- a never-ending vicious circle. An unfortunate thing aside is that what is excluded in this entire procedure is an acceptance of their real self. Narcissists do not understand who they are.

Maybe much more unexpected is that narcissists will cause personal attacks. Their pomposity welcomes-- no, beg for-- criticism and assault on their character by others; people simply ache to be the ones to offer narcissists their punishment.

When dealing with the narcissist, it works to remember that below that veneer of arrogant confidence lies a narcissistic injury. It does not take much to gain access to this wound. Thus, your narcissist can be quickly hurt and embarrassed by insults, rejections, and minor criticisms.

Exercises: Does the Person in Your Life Have a Narcissistic Wound?

Each of the following statements describes how a narcissist may be wounded. Fill in the blanks using a scale of 1 to 5:

1. He or she seems to be overly delicate.

2. This person gets mad when you disagree with him or her.

3. She or he can never be wrong.

4. When you try to give positive criticism, he or she gets upset or sulks even.

5. He or she appears to need consistent peace of mind.

6. He or she always seems to be fishing for compliments.

7. If somebody has disagreed with or slammed him or her, this person will rant and rage.

8. Often she or he looks like a wounded little kid.

9. The criticism appears to stun him or her.

10. This person will cut another individual out of his or her life the minute that an individual disagrees or finds fault with him or her.

11. She or he never forgets a slight.

12. She or he counterattacks swiftly.

13. This person is continuously saying how wonderful she or he is as if needing this self-reinforcement.

14. This person becomes secured or protective when discussing his or her weaknesses.

15. You feel that you need to pick your words thoroughly, or you will offend him or her in some way.

Now add up the rating. A score of 52 or above recommends that this person has a narcissistic wound.

Now list some examples of how the person in your life has exhibited a narcissistic wound:

Take another moment for reflection. Knowing that this person suffers from a narcissistic injury can go a long way in your handling situations with him. You will not blame yourself when he overacts-- it's not your fault that he goes into rages. You will comprehend why it is so difficult for him to admit that he is wrong, for doing so only strengthens the idea that he is defective. You will know his need to denigrate others. You also will grow to acknowledge that you will get forward with the narcissist by addressing the hurt underneath the anger. Suppose your narcissistic spouse is in a tirade because you spent too much time speaking with an attractive salesclerk. Instead of saying something like, "You always accuse me of doing things that I have not done," you can say something like, "I'm so sorry I hurt you. I didn't want it to look like I was flirting. That wouldn't be reasonable to you." You will discover that this type of statement will go a long way in helping you to handle your relationship.

After reading this chapter, your perceptions and interpretations of issues have most likely changed. Interactions that have baffled you in the past must now be making more sense. What is the most essential thing that you will take away from this chapter? How will you react differently to the person in your life when she displays the traits talked about here?

At this moment you ought to have a relatively great idea whether the person with whom you are in a relationship is narcissistic

CHAPTER FOUR

Narcissism in Personal Relationships

Narcissistic people can be discovered in all strolls of life. You can find them in your neighborhood, your school, your business, and, yes, even your household. You might find them on the front page of the paper or your TV screen, however, it's when the narcissist gets close and personal that the sparks begin to fly. Having a narcissistic spouse, employer, friend, or relative can be stressful. And each type of relationship brings its unique difficulties. This chapter will cover narcissistic romantic relationships: We wish to note here that although you must focus on the kind of relationship that is affecting you the most, you ought to check out the others too. The majority of the accurate information, advice, and exercises provided here can be used in a spectrum of relationship types.

Narcissists in Romantic Relationships

We would like to begin this section of the book by being absolutely and painfully blunt, so here goes: No one is more at risk when handling a narcissist than someone who's involved in a long-lasting romantic relationship with a narcissist. Within an intimate relationship, the narcissist has a bounty of opportunities across scores of personal interactions to do hurt to a genuine, dedicated, and so susceptible lover. Even by the most basic of definitions, intimacy needs that you clear away a part of yourself to make room for another. Consider it. To be able to vibrate with the feelings of our loved ones is a character requirement for anybody involved with a dedicated relationship. The total intake of the narcissist with his own needs makes him the odds-on preferred to disregard the demands of his partner continuously. Indeed, several narcissists love withholding the very thing their partner needs the most; this is a type of one-upmanship developed to keep those around them humbled.

It is easy to be misled by a narcissist. He naturally predicts an attractive guise of charisma, status, confidence, and appeal.

In the beginning, the narcissist will amaze you by meeting all of your romantic dreams in a whirlwind of love. The lovemaking is enthusiastic and intense; she will do everything she can to satisfy and impress you. He'll take you to must-see concerts and the trendiest restaurants, to the most expensive and significant nightspots and Broadway plays. He'll honor your birthday with an extravagant event and luxurious gifts. Heck, he'll celebrate your mother's birthday with expensive presents. ("Isn't he only terrific? Now there's the man you must marry!") He will write you love letters instilled with statements of his eternal commitment to you, rivaling the poetry of the masters: you are his true love. He will make compilations of your favorite music. He will mesmerize you for nights on end with his creative and witty jokes and his captivating stories of action-packed adventures.

The narcissist might have been attracted to you because she thought that you improved her image in some way, or she saw you as someone who was as terrific as she was.

Even as early as the courtship stage, nevertheless, you might have noticed that your partner tended to control the discussion a little frequently, boast a lot, and become extremely animated when talking about himself, which he always had to overcome someone. Start talking about yourself, and he began to look in the other directions, a process referred to as "glazing over".

For the narcissist, it is all about using you for his needs while sucking you dry. The narcissist is a vampire on an unlimited journey to drain pipes the energy out of others. He is always hunting for somebody to meet his needs, to fill the vacuum inside, to verify him as somebody who is matchless and extraordinary, and to pump up his deflated self-esteem. The narcissist needs someone to applaud her achievements, to honor her cleverness; you are a unique kind of confidant and one of the few in the world who can understand and appreciate her uniqueness. She needs you to join her in valuing all the beautiful things in life, to value her expert tastes in music, art, fashion, style, and so on. Or he needs you to tell him that he's the most elegant enthusiast on the planet which nobody could satisfy you the way that he does. Or possibly the narcissist just needs a whipping young boy, somebody to blame and to put his frustrations on-- somebody to take the fall for the emptiness he feels.

When the narcissist discovers that you cannot be his fantasy-- no human being on earth might-- he will go back on the hunt, which he never gave up. Narcissists are well-known for secretly keeping all their alternatives open; they are always looking for a much better deal, a much better relationship. Commitment is an abomination. Better to leave all choices available.

CHAPTER FIVE

Difference Between Narcissism and Egocentrism

We see the world from the inside out-- a reality that leads everyone to be self-centered. The technical term for this is "egocentrism.".

As a cognitive bias, egocentrism describes the natural restriction on our empathetic caused by the easy fact that we can just see the world from our viewpoint. It takes a special effort to see the world from any perspective aside from through our eyes.

The fundamental egocentrism developed into our cognitive apparatus became an essential part of Swiss psychologist Jean Piaget's theory about kid advancement. In observing kids explain the way a small table-sized design of a mountain may look to someone else, Piaget found that before the age of our two, this seemingly simple job was remarkably challenging.

Young kids seem cognitively unable to take the perspective of another person. This truth, by the way, makes them easy to beat at a two-person perspective game such as checkers. They can't imagine what the board looks like to you, and as a result, will make mistakes caused by their assumptions that you see what they see.

Although we all outgrow this stage of development, even adults find it difficult to conquer the cognitive kind of egocentrism entirely. You can prove this with a straightforward experiment of yourself.

Take a skill that you have at a well-experienced job that you can quickly do effectively. Now, try to explain that work to somebody who's never tried the job at all. Consider something as essential as making a cup of coffee or hammering a nail. Or imagine something more complex such as preserving a computer system file, establishing a printer, or beginning on email. Whatever the task, imagine that your job is to tell somebody how to do it.

The majority of people find it difficult to handle the view of someone who knows nothing about this well-mastered ability. Even if you think you're great at laying out the actions in this job that comes so fast to you, possibilities are that you will not be able to eliminate your knowledge of the task or memory of the actions needed to bring it out before you can teach it to anybody else.

We don't ever ultimately grow out of the youthful form of egocentrism called the fictional audience. If you've used up a new sport or chosen to start learning how to dance, you may have often felt that everybody's eyes were on you as you fell or just looked awkward. Feeling that everyone is looking at you, the embarrassment becomes excessive.

What you fail to know is that everybody else feels similarly awkward and ashamed. In truth, they're not taking a look at you at all because they're so worried about their performance. As Ann Landers once mentioned, "At age 20, we worry about what others believe of us. At 40, we do not care what they think about us. At 60, we discover they haven't been thinking about us at all."

Some types of narcissism might come hard-wired into the person's character. Nurture can defeat nature due to narcissism's incredibly reinforcing properties. Simply as numerous entitled narcissists are reproduced, not born, into their exploitative habits. Let's take the example of people who are late in situations that inconvenience other people. The latecomers can see, from their perspective, why they're late. They know that traffic was terrible, that they had one last email to answer, or that they could not extricate themselves from a conversation.

Gradually, chronic latecomers might start to experience some benefit from their delay, which just serves to reinforce their tendency to be late. This is how the arrogant propensity to be late can create. Like the star who flounces in to inhabit spotlight in the middle of a crowded scene, the latecomer sweeps in and becomes the center of everyone's attention. When the latecomer encounters no unfavorable consequences, and when the situations need the person to be there for things to start, the propensity is reinforced even further.

Imagine everybody at a birthday party waiting on the honoree. The party can't get underway until she or he arrives. The doorbell rings 30 minutes later on, and the crowd can now welcome the birthday young boy or lady. They might feel resentful; the guests nevertheless strengthen the person's lateness because no one wants to reveal their annoyance openly. Similarly, in charge, which shows up 5 minutes late for a meeting, can also be ensured of a grand entrance without implications. None of the employees can complain out loud about this disrespect, so the boss sees no reason to change and, in reality, might be even later for the next conference.

It's straightforward to slip from common egocentrism to entitled narcissism. Without encountering any adverse consequences, people such as chronic latecomers see no reason to change their habits. No one complains, no job is lost, and all they get are the rewards of drawing everybody's attention.

The issue is exaggerated amongst people who slowly get public acknowledgment. Stars, musicians, reality show contestants, and politicians who start to get the eye of the media are especially vulnerable to taking on egotistical tendencies. If they do not remain grounded in their previous truth, they can become victims of the narcissistic bubble in which they lose their sense of accountability for their behavior. The grand entrance becomes nearly a required part of their job and if they're not careful, it can lead them to take on an entitled mindset toward their loved ones.

What's going on inside the mind and emotions of entitled narcissists? They might not even be mindful of the hatred they're developing amongst their closest and dearest if they've slipped into this pattern of habits accidentally through the reinforcement process.

At the same time, as their narcissism advances, they might find that their self-confidence becomes more and more reliant on having that position in the spotlight. They now want it like a drug when having been the center of everybody's look. To protect their increasingly unstable sense of personality, they need to surround themselves with admirers who will prop them up. They feel insignificant if they go unnoticed amongst a crowd of strangers. Unlike their celeb friends who love going undercover, media stars who enter the conceited bubble discover it tough to exist without being followed by paparazzi.

Ordinary people who've developed the entitled type of narcissism can be just as empty and shrank as the celebrity icon. Their emotional lives are being dominated by the need to be known, and they got progressively out of their way to guarantee this need is pleased. They firmly insist on receiving special treatment, complain when they don't get it, and decline people who they feel get in their way. Anyone who grumbles, for instance, about their persistent lateness, is eliminated from their list of staff members or friends.

Understanding the dangers of letting egocentrism leave control, how can you participate in vital action? Whether it's you or a loved one you're trying to assist, here are five guidelines:

- **Make an honest assessment of your egocentric behaviors.**

Take stock of the behaviors caused by ordinary egocentrism that might be leaving control. Whether it's persistent lateness or poorly conceived Facebook posts, decide whether you're letting your internal perspective change your social interactions.

- **Check how other people feel.**

Have a look at how other people are feeling by putting yourself in their shoes. Using active, compassionate listening, for instance, you can expand your viewpoint to see not just from the inside out, but from the outside in.

- **Develop your inner sense of self.**

Do not allow your self-definition to be too reliant on getting attention from others. Find ways to develop your self-confidence by establishing internal standards that enable you to reward yourself for your actual achievements.

- **Squelch your fictional audience.**

You may feel that everybody is looking at you and judging you, but in reality, a lot of people are just as worried about themselves as they are about you. If you commit a social mistake, it's not likely that it's as noticed (and criticized) as you think it is.

- **Practice counter-egocentrism.**

Test out your abilities to take another person's perspective by trying to discuss your skill to someone who's never attempted the job in question. Read over your emails before you send them to make sure you have not skipped over details that only you understand. Include other people in your in-jokes with your friends.

No matter where you are on the egocentrism-narcissism dimension, you can pull yourself back toward a frame of mind that will enable you to see yourself as others see you. When you do, you'll find that you can live more healthily and separately based on a more vital and internally based on a sense of self.

Egocentric vs. Narcissistic

Since the term egocentric describes someone who is self-focused and not able to imagine any other viewpoint than their own, you might wonder if this is the same thing as narcissism. Although there are some parallels, there is a distinct distinction between narcissistic and egocentric personalities.

A few of the resemblances between egocentric and conceited include:

-Concentrate on own understanding and viewpoint Absence of empathy

-Failure to recognize the needs of others

-Excessive thoughts of how others might see them

-Decision-making around the needs of self

In addition to these traits, nevertheless, narcissist people also demonstrate:

-Excessive demand for acknowledgment and appreciation

-View self as extraordinarily deserving or important

-Sense of entitlement

-Manipulate others to get what they want

-Arrogant and pompous behaviors

-Preoccupied with dreams of unrestricted success, power, or charm

The main distinction between being egocentric and narcissistic is that somebody who is egotistical always seeks admiration from others with a need to feel essential and valued.

Remember that all of us might have egotistical and egocentric propensities. Still, specific criteria need to be met for someone to have a scientific medical diagnosis of narcissist personality disorder.

-Effect.

Egocentric people can find it tough to relate with others or maintain significant relationships for a long period. The predisposition toward self can result in an egocentric individual having a hard time at home, at work, and within their intimate relationships.

The primary reason for these battles is the absence of the ability to see or understand somebody's perspective aside from their own. As you can think of, this might negatively impact things like:

-Trust.

Nearness or intimacy.

Emotional attunement.

Decision making.

Collaboration.

Teamwork.

It can be unnoticeable or feel that you have no voice when spending time with them; it can be tough to be around somebody who is egocentric.

Some of the ways being around selfish people might affect us include feelings of:

-**Low Self-Worth**: When we feel unimportant, we are left feeling low as if our opinions don't matter.

-**Self-Doubt**: You might question your judgment or understanding.

-**Confusion**: You might ask if the person acknowledges their egocentric ways.

-**Sadness**: You might pity the person or sad for yourself after communicating with them.

-**Anger**: It can be hard to practice assertiveness with a selfish person, which can lead to disappointment and anger over not feeling seen or heard.

-**Bitterness**: After a time, you may find yourself bitter toward them for the ways they behave and how you feel after interactions.

-**Detachment**: Unfortunately, if the pattern continues, you may want to move far from the person as much as you can to safeguard your sense of self.

There might be times when you can just choose to limit your exposure to a selfish person; nevertheless, there are many circumstances in which it is not an option, and you have to discover how to look after yourself while in their presence.

Egocentrics in Relationships.

For the egocentric person, life can be isolating and anxiety-producing. When dealing with cognitive bias, an egocentric person might think that all eyes are on them and that others notice every move or decision they make.

This can produce a remarkable quantity of pressure for that person, causing anxiety around their decision making and social interactions. When they want to link with others, they may not know how to do that or might make efforts to connect and become confused as to why their actions don't work.

To be in a relationship with somebody who is egocentric can be lonesome, and you may feel you are never seen, heard, or valued in the relationship.

Your partner may make crucial decisions without you, make plans based on their needs and schedule, or seem uninterested or far-off if you come to them with an emotional need for comfort, encouragement, or reassurance. The egocentric partner may think that the relationship is delicate when their partner is frequently left feeling invisible and devalued.

Common Egocentric Traits.

It is common for a lot of people to have some level of egocentrism. Research study has revealed that grownups tend to have egocentric shortcomings in the following methods:

-False Consensus Effect: When we overstate just how much other people share our point of view or choices. We tend to think that others would concur with us or see things our way.

-Abuse of Knowledge: When those who are professionals in their field tend to talk above people around them on that subject. They forget that there is a difference between the levels of knowledge they have on the subject compared to those around them.

-Impression of Transparency: When people feel that others can see their emotions in an accessible experience. For example, we might think that others can see how nervous we feel when we are giving a presentation at work.

-Spotlight Effect: When people overstate how much others are noticing their presence or habits. We might stroll into a room and feel like people are enjoying our every move when, in truth, they are delicately engaging with each other and might not notice us at all.

How to Become Less Egocentric

Because we all have a selfish slant to some extent, we can all gain from softening our egocentric edge. Being self-centered can be an advantage when we are trying to maintain our values or when we are feeling disrespected.

Nevertheless, when an egocentric frame of mind starts to impact our daily habits, adversely, it can cause issues. There are practical suggestions for becoming less egocentric.

- **Decrease.**

In some cases, we make choices out of fear. Fear likes to pressure us and require us to think in a much "flight or battle" way, even when we are not in the existence of a threat. Falling can help you clarify what it is that needs to be decided, thinking about how your decision might affect those around you.

- **Look around.**

We like to believe that life is all about us. There are people around us who care and want to be a part of our lives and choice making. Look around and see who is waiting for you and be ready to assist.

- **Gamble.**

Often people end up being more egocentric because they have discovered through experience that they cannot rely on others to be there for them. As you look around and observe who is waiting for you, take the possibility to let somebody show you what they can do. Not just are you practicing walking through your worries but allowing someone who cares about you to get close.

- **Stay present.**

Just as some egocentric people have learned not to trust others, some have discovered never to show vulnerability. Even if you decide and someone notices a misstep, keep moving. All of us want to live well, and it not comfortable when others see our mistakes. Staying present allows you to practice navigating uncomfortable situations, learning that you can pass through them, and still be okay.

CHAPTER SIX

How do you Change in Response to the Narcissist in your Life

For each of the following statements, check off whether the situation rarely explained, often, frequently, or always happens to you.

1. You find yourself taking a rear seat to the narcissist's desires or wants, thereby forgoing your own:

- **rarely happens**
- **sometimes happens**
- **frequently happens**
- **always happens**

2. When something fails, the narcissist blames you for whatever the issue might be, and as a result, you are concerned and on guard about making mistakes.

- **rarely happens**
- **sometimes happens**

- **frequently happens**
- **always happens**

3. Because the narcissist typically discounts your opinions or how you feel, you find yourself concealing your feelings or thoughts.

- **rarely happens**
- **sometimes happens**
- **frequently happens**
- **always happens**

4. You discover that the narcissist uses your head, energy, or ideas for his or her gain or will have you do things that she or he dislikes doing.

As a result, you discover yourself being emotionally withholding or distancing in the relationship.

- **rarely happens**
- **sometimes happens**
- **frequently happens**
- **always happens**

5. You find yourself wanting to reinforce the narcissist's ego or deal reassurance. When you do not want to, you will express admiration also. This makes you feel resentful.

- **rarely happens**
- **sometimes happens**
- **frequently happens**
- **always happens**

6. Because you're afraid that you'll be told you're being self-centered or requiring, you avoid asking things of the narcissist.

- **rarely happens**
- **sometimes happens**
- **frequently happens**
- **always happens**

7. You forgo making plans to do something for yourself because you feel you're at the narcissist's beck and call.

- **rarely happens**
- **sometimes happens**

- **frequently happens**
- **always happens**

8. When they criticize him or her, you discover yourself needing to defend the narcissist to others.

- **rarely happens**
- **sometimes happens**
- **frequently happens**
- **always happens**

9. Because you're scared, you may be embarrassed by what the narcissist may say or do, you find yourself avoiding social engagements with the narcissist.

- **rarely happens**
- **sometimes happens**
- **frequently happens**
- **always happens**

10. You avoid gatherings with the narcissist because of how the narcissist treats you when you're around other people, and you don't wish to feel humiliated.

- **rarely happens**
- **sometimes happens**
- **frequently happens**
- **always happens**

Now take a look at your actions to the questions. If you've responded " often happens" or "constantly occurs" to more than six of these questions, then you probably are being stressed by your relationship with a narcissist. You likely discover yourself asking whether the relationship will ever be compatible or whether your needs will ever be met.

The next workout will assist you in starting a journal of your responses and responses to various scenarios that may arise day-to-day with the narcissist in your life.

Understanding What You Can and Cannot Change

This part concentrates on helping you develop new techniques for handling the narcissist in your life. You are probably excited to start because the ways that you've used before have not worked effectively. But before you go any further, it's essential to have sensible expectations of what you can and cannot change.

What you are likely to change is not the narcissist himself. You shouldn't expect the narcissist in your life to change for your sake, and for some factors, narcissists are ordinarily unlikely to change by themselves.

Narcissists Do Not Know They Are Narcissists

One of the reasons that narcissists are unlikely to change is that they don't know they are narcissists. They lack self-insight. They do not see themselves the way others see them, and they don't understand how frustrating their behaviors are to others.

It's extensively accepted that teenagers will typically act narcissistically, which the teenage years might be an attempting time for parents. Thankfully, the majority of teenagers outgrow their narcissistic behavior as they begin to establish a more profound sense of compassion for others. Those who do not, nevertheless, will become grownups who have the same sense of self-entitlement and absence of empathy. A narcissist might feel he is empathic by stepping over the homeless person on the pathway and not stepping on him. Likewise, if you ask a narcissist to change a behavior that bothers you, he will not have the empathy to respond constructively.

Keep in mind that someone with full-blown NPD is going to be more difficult and resistant to change than somebody who shows only periodic episodes of egocentric habits. Thankfully, the techniques in this book can be applied to anybody who shows narcissistic qualities.

Lack of self-insight is a characteristic that people with character conditions have in common, and it's a problem that all narcissists share, to a greater or lower extent. This lack of insight just serves to fuel the narcissistic habits. There may be instances where a narcissist comes face-to-face with his addictions, but these moments are fleeting.

Narcissists Are Unlikely to Change

Another particular common to all character conditions that make change hard for the narcissist is that these characteristics are frequently long-standing and are for that reason neither transient nor easily changed. Imagine changing from being right-handed to left-handed. If you were a political conservative all your adult life and then tried to alter to become a liberal (or vice versa), envision. So too, for the narcissist, it's practically incomprehensible to picture modification. Neither would she see the need for change. In the after-effects of a relationship break up or even a marital separation, a narcissist would probably enter counseling only if court purchased or forced into it and, even then, would likely give herself as the victim or injured party, as if to say, "How could he or she have done this to me?" The narcissist is not likely to go into counseling to analyze how her habits might have contributed to the relationship's end.

Why Therapy or Counseling May Not Help

Did you ever hear the old joke, "How many therapists does it take to change a light bulb?" Response: "One, however, the light bulb should want to change."

Therapy and counseling are enough for people who wish to change. Truth be told, treatment is less reliable or ineffective with people who desire no part of change, and this is as real for narcissists as it is for anybody getting therapy. In instances where people are court-mandated into psychotherapy or counseling, it seems the best we can do as counselors are to arouse their hunger for change or try to tip the balance for those who might be ambivalent about change. Some people really need to strike bottom before they even start to consider the notion that it's they who need to change, not those around them. This problem is commonly seen with alcoholics and drug abusers, who frequently must strike bottom before they can start to see that it is their drinking or usage of drugs that are producing the issues in their relationships and lives.

It's often believed that therapy alone will remedy any egotistical and egocentric habits. Moms and dads often feel that if they can just get their belligerent teen to opt for counseling, she will be able to talk out her anger. Lots of partners of narcissists think that if they can just get their companion to go to therapy, it will turn him into a compassionate human being. Here's the problem: the narcissist should be ready personally in the process of treatment or counseling for it to work.

A partner's want to go into counseling can be a favorable action, but if that partner is not thinking about change, he will not change. For instance, it is an accepted practice not to treat couples when abuse is present in the relationship. The reason is that the batterer will often use things the partner exposes in counseling as a further reason to batter. We also don't mean to say that all narcissists are evil, vicious, and computing. The point is that therapeutic change begins with inspiration and a desire to confront uneasy aspects of oneself. Unfortunately, narcissism often works against the narcissist when it comes to benefit from therapy, as is highlighted in the following case.

-Your partner only used you for sex.

Your partner needed you to provide satisfaction in his/her life (or to join him or her in pursuing drama and pleasure).

Exploitation is among the critical symptoms of narcissism; being used is one of the threats of being involved with a narcissist. He will always take advantage of you in some way if your partner is narcissistic. If you rebuff these efforts, he will start to see you as a less viable partner; a process psychologists call decrease.

Things You Can Change

The secret to improving your relationship with the narcissist is to take a look at what you can change about your responses. You can do the following: shed your rejection about the narcissist and how he affects you; stop believing that the narcissist's habits have to do with you; detach with love and take much better care of yourself.

-Shed Your Denial

It's typical for people who are handling narcissists to be taken in by their charm, their high self-esteem, and their ability to work for the crowd. Simply put, it's simple to be in denial as to what you're dealing with.

The Process of Devaluation

Soon after the courtship is over, narcissists generally begin to become disillusioned with their romantic partners. As the relationship progresses and the narcissist discovers more factual information about you, he will find that you are the human and not the goddess he at first saw you as. This can be devastating for the narcissist; you, in all your humanness, will not be able to be her equal, will never have the ability to relate with, and appreciate his unique type of genius. The narcissist begins, then, to find fault with you, initially asking you to "lose some weight," "cut your hair," "dress more like your girlfriend," "stop distracting me when I speak," or all of the above. But as time goes on, the attacks become more vitriolic and lengthy: you are "nothing but a clingy kid," "fat, unsightly and stupid," "a shame and are holding me back from my destiny of reputation and fortune," or "the worst mistake I ever made in my life." Or "You disgust me. You'll speak with my lawyers." Yup, devaluation can be a little rough on your self-esteem.

At this moment, the narcissist has reversed the switch and shut off his feelings for you. He may have already discovered another person to pursue. Narcissists love the act of seduction, and many will not commit to a relationship, for they love falling in love-- it's a day-to-day repair-- but are incapable of doing the real work of keeping a genuinely intimate bond.

The stings of decline can be painful, but keep in mind that they are lies used by the narcissist to preserve his self-esteem. And keep in mind, it is also a lie when the narcissist sees you as best. It is seductive and envigorating certainly when the narcissist puts you up on a pedestal by misestimating you. But, like any drug, the hangover of devaluation soon follows. The apparent lesson here might be not to consume in the overvaluation in the first place.

Know That Narcissism Is Not About You

Once again, many people get caught in the trap of believing that they are to blame for the narcissist's behavior or inability to love others. They might sign up for the belief that if they loved her more, or if they did exactly what he desired, the narcissist would ultimately come around and have the ability to love or be there for them. The point deserves repeating: You didn't cause it.

You can't change it. You can't manage it.

You will have made a significant change in your approach to the narcissistic behavior when you realize this.

Keep in mind, however, that narcissists are quite proficient at pressing blame for their behavior onto others. Given their hidden low self-esteem, they have trouble accepting responsibility when things go wrong or do not go as they planned. You have to be vigilant about not blaming yourself when the narcissist attempts to blame you.

Detach with Love

Detaching with love is an idea that came from Al-Anon: that you could detach from an alcoholic's habits and attitudes while not shutting the person out totally or shutting off your love for him. Detachment is naturally much more challenging to bring out in everyday life than it sounds.

First, you must be ready and able to identify narcissistic behavior in the other person (such as when she is acting big-headed, haughty, or entitled, or is requiring unique treatment or attention).

Secondly, you should be able to accept that these habits and mindsets become part of narcissism.

Third, you should be able to take the truth that this belongs to the narcissist's nature. This would be similar to the spouse of an alcoholic who instead of trying to determine why the alcoholic just went on a three-day binge, would accept that this is what alcoholics do: they drink.

Since detachment is easier stated than done, it might be beneficial to give you with a few examples of what detachment from a narcissist may look like. Here are some sample dialogues, beginning with what a narcissist may say to you and followed by how you might react in a more detached way.

Narcissist: Can't you do anything? I'm stuck continuously doing everything around here!

You: I guess you're right, I'm not best.

Narcissist: (Talks while standing in line at a restaurant.) I can't believe we're not being seated right away. Didn't you make the bookings?

You: Yes, I made them for 7:00 p.m. Maybe you must make the reservations next time instead of me.

Narcissist: I can't believe we're lost again. It's your fault!

You: I don't feel I'm to blame. Let's stop somewhere so you can ask directions from somebody.

Narcissist: You always take too long to get ready when we are going out. I've had it.

You: Maybe you should go on ahead of me given that you're ready, and I'll meet you there.

Narcissist: Maybe you should give me $100, so I can go out with my good friends. You owe it to me.

You: Sorry. I do not have the cash to loan to you today.

In being detached, you're neither accepting the blame that the narcissist might be trying to load on you nor reacting defensively. The eliminated person, in essence, is saying, "Because you think you're always right, and I'm always wrong, there's no point in arguing with you, is there?" Detaching with love doesn't mean you need to become robotic and unfeeling or disinterested; it just means that you're no longer reacting to narcissistic behavior or attitudes.

Take Better Care of Yourself

Many people who stay in the controls of a narcissist often find themselves waiting for some benefit that never appears to be upcoming. Narcissists are more typically so soaked up with themselves and their agendas that they never look to navigate to make good on commitments. Whether it be the narcissistic manager who guarantees his employee a raise or the narcissistic parent who promises to show up at her child's school play or the narcissistic friend who does not show up for a lunch date, the style is comparable: the narcissist fails to deliver.

You can't make the narcissist come through for you, but what you can do is take better care of yourself. A staff member working for a narcissistic boss discovers to look after herself or to get her requirements fulfilled in other places. Kids who grow up with a narcissistic mom and dad find out to find other adults they can rely on. Having a friend who is a narcissist is typically like not having a friend at all. Taking much better care of yourself can start with a lowering of your expectations of this person.

You can begin to take better care of yourself by looking at other ways to get your needs met. Who are people you can rely on? Are there ways you can treat yourself much better instead of expecting something that your narcissist may not be willing or able to give?

Exercise: Treating Yourself Better

Mention people in your life who you feel you can count on:

Now make a list of things you can do to treat yourself better or ways to get your needs met without having to depend on the narcissist in your life:

Fantastic job! You've just begun to emancipate yourself from narcissistic habits.

Reduced Expectations or Affordable Expectations?

You've likely heard the contexture meaning of madness: when you do the same thing but expect a different result. It may be nuts to expect a narcissist to change when the result is always a disappointment, but this is all frequently what people near to a narcissist continue to do. It's simple to get caught in the expectation that the narcissist can be various or that he will change. As gone over previously, this is partially due to the truth that sometimes a narcissist will appear to muster some degree of empathy or heat or what appears to be caring feelings. Still, usually, these moments either are short-term or represent feigned habits.

As you embark on the challenge of changing yourself and your approach to the narcissist in your life, here are some suggestions for keeping things in viewpoint:

1. Don't expect the narcissist to change.

2. Don't expect reliable warmth or love from the narcissist.

3. Don't expect praise or appreciation from the narcissist.

4. Do not expect the narcissist to support you (particularly in times of need) or to support your development.

5. Expect that the narcissist will try to take advantage of you or exploit you.

6. Expect your narcissist to go to any lengths to build herself up, even if it means belittling you, criticizing you, or putting you down.

7. Expect the narcissist to assume you will treat him as distinct or unique.

As you ponder these ideas, consider whether you will be able to use each in your life.

CHAPTER SEVEN

Spotting Toxic People and Defending Yourself from Emotional Abuse

Your strengthened intuition is the best defense against a manipulative person. It is an ability that can never be exploited-- and as soon as discovered, it will serve you a lifetime.

Thirty Red Flags

There are a lot of great research studies on the characteristics and qualities of psychopaths. What's different when it comes to this list? Well, for one, it's specifically about relationships. It's likewise about you. Each point needs introspection and self-awareness. You cannot focus entirely on their habits-- that's just half the battle if you want to spot toxic people. You need to also know the looming warnings in your own heart. You will be ready for anything.

1. **Gaslighting and crazy-making.** When confronted with it, they blatantly deny their manipulative habits and neglect evidence. If you try to disprove their fabrications with truths, they end up being dismissive and crucial. Instead of them resolving their inappropriate habits, in some way, always becomes your fault for being "superficial" and "crazy." Toxic people condition you to think that the problem isn't the abuse itself, but instead your reactions to their abuse.

2. **Cannot put themselves in your shoes, or anybody else's, for that matter**. You find yourself frantically trying to discuss how they may feel if you were treating them this way, and they just look at you blankly. You gradually find out not to disclose with your feelings with them, because you're typically met with silence or annoyance.

3. **The critical pretender**. "Do as I say, not as I do." They have high expectations for love, fidelity, and respect. After the idealization stage, they will give none of this back to you. They will cheat, lie, slam, and control. But you are expected to remain

perfect; otherwise, you will immediately be changed and considered unstable.

4. **Pathological lying and reasons**. There is always an excuse for everything, even things that don't need explanation. They tell lies faster than you can ask them. They continuously blame others-- it is never their fault. They spend more time justifying their behavior than improving it. Even when captured in a lie, they express no regret or embarrassment. Usually, it almost seems as if they wanted you to catch them.

5. **Focus on your mistakes and overlooks their own**. If they are two hours late, don't forget that you were once five minutes late to your first date. If you explain their improper habits, they will always fast to turn the conversation back on you. You might begin to embrace perfectionist qualities, really conscious that any mistake can and will be utilized against you.

6. **You find yourself explaining the standard components of human respect to a full-grown man or lady.** Typical people

understand fundamental principles like sincerity and generosity. Psychopaths typically appear to be innocent and childish but do not let this mask fool you. No grownup ought to be told how she or he is making other people feel.

7. **Selfishness and a crippling thirst for attention**. They drain pipes the energy from you and consume your whole life. Their need for adoration is pressing. You thought you were the only person who could make them happy, and now you feel that anyone with a pounding pulse could fit the role. Nevertheless, the reality is: nobody can fill the deep space of a psychopath's soul.

8. **Accuses you of being emotional that they are purposefully annoying**. They call you envious after blatantly flirting with an ex-- over social media for the whole world to see. They call you clingy after purposefully neglecting you for days on end. They use your produced reactions to gather sympathy from other targets, trying to prove how "hysterical" you've become. You most likely considered yourself to be an extremely easygoing

person, but an encounter with a psychopath will (briefly) turn that idea upside down.

9. **You find yourself playing detective**. It's never occurred in any other relationship, but unexpectedly you're investigating the person you once trusted unconditionally. If they're active on Facebook, you begin scrolling back years on their albums and posts. Same with their ex. You're looking for responses to a feeling you can't rather say.

10. **You are the only person who sees their real colors**. No matter what they do, they always appear to have a fan club cheering for them. The narcissist uses these people for cash, resources, and attention-- but the fan club won't discover, because this individual strategically distracts them with shallow appreciation. Toxic can keep superficial relationships far longer than relationships.

11. **You fear that any battle could be your last**. Regular couples argue to deal with problems, but psychopaths make it clear that

negative discussions will jeopardize the relationship, specifically ones regarding their behavior. Any of your efforts to improve interaction will typically result in the quiet treatment. You say sorry and forgive quickly, otherwise, you know they'll lose interest in you.

12. **Slowly and steadily deteriorates your borders**. They slam you with a condescending, joking sort of mindset. They smirk when you try to show yourself. Teasing ends up being the primary mode of communication in your relationship. They subtly belittle your intelligence and capabilities.

They call you insane and delicate if you point this out. You might start to feel resentful and upset, but you find out to press away those feelings in favor of keeping the peace.

13. **They expect you to read their mind. If they stop communicating with you for some days, it's your fault for not understanding the plans they didn't tell you about**. There will always be an excuse that makes them be the victim to support

this. They make crucial decisions about the relationship, and they notify everyone other than you.

14. **You feel on edge around this person, but you still want them to like you**. You find yourself writing off the majority of their questionable behavior as insensitive or accidental since you're in continuous competitors with others for their attention and appreciation. They don't appear to care when you leave their side-- they can just as fast proceed to the next source of energy.

15. **An unusual variety of "crazy" people in their past**. Any ex-lover or friend who did not come crawling back to them will likely be identified envious, an alcoholic, or some other nasty smear. Make no mistake: they will talk about you the same way to their next target.

16. **Provokes jealousy and competitions while preserving their cover of blamelessness**. They once directed all their attention to you, which makes it explicitly puzzling when they start to

withdraw and focus on other people. They do things that regularly make you question your place in their heart. If they're active on social media, they'll draw formerly knocked exes with old songs, images, and inside jokes. They take care of the "competitors" activity and neglect yours.

17. **Compares you to every other person in their life**. They compare you to ex-lovers, friends, relatives, and your eventual replacement. When romanticizing, they make you feel unique by telling you how much better you are than these people. When devaluing, they use these comparisons to make you feel inferior and jealous.

18. **The quality they once declared to appreciate about you suddenly become glaring faults**. At first, they interest your inmost vulnerabilities and vanities, observing and simulating precisely what they think you wish to hear. But after you're hooked, they begin to use these things against you. You invest more and more time trying to show yourself worthwhile to the same person who once said you were perfect.

19. **Cracks in their mask**. There are fleeting moments when the charming, innocent person is replaced by something else. You see a side to them that didn't come out throughout the fantasy stage, and it is a side that's cold, inconsiderate, and manipulative. You begin to see that their personality just does not add up-- that the person you fell in love with does not seems to exist.

20. **Quickly tired**. They are continuously surrounded by other people, promoted and applauded at all times. They can't tolerate being alone for an extended period. They become easily distracted by anything that doesn't directly affect them thrillingly or favorably. Firstly, you might think they're worldly and exciting, and you feel inferior for preferring familiarity and consistency.

21. **Triangulation**. They surround themselves with former enthusiasts, prospective mates, and anyone else who gives them added attention. This consists of people that the narcissist might have formerly denounced and declared you superior to. This

makes you feel confused and produces the perception that the toxic is in high demand at any time.

22. **Covert abuse**. At an early age, many of us were taught to determine physical mistreatment and outright verbal insults, but with narcissists, the violence is not so apparent. You likely won't even comprehend that you were in a violent relationship until long after it's over. Through personalized fantasy and indirect decline, a narcissist can efficiently deteriorate the identity of any selected target. From a stranger's perspective, you will seem to have "lost it," while the narcissist calmly leaves, totally unharmed.

23. **Pity plays, and sympathy stories**. Their bad behavior constantly has sob- story roots. They claim to act this way because of an abusive ex, an abusive moms and dad, or an abusive feline. They state that all they've ever desired is some solitude. They say they dislike drama-- and yet there's more drama surrounding them than anyone you've ever known.

24. **The mean and sweet cycle**. Often they shower you with attention, in some cases they disregard and condemn you, often. They treat you differently in public than they do when they are behind the closed doors. They might be speaking about marriage one day and breaking up the next day. You never know your stand with them.

25. **This person becomes your whole life**. You're spending most of your time with them and their friends, and less time with your support network. They're all you talk and think about anymore. You isolate yourself to make sure you're available for them. You cancel plans and excitedly wait by the phone for their next call. For some reason, the relationship appears to involve a lot of sacrifices on your end, but just a few on theirs.

26. **Conceit**. Despite the pure, sweet image they provided in the early phases, you begin to notice an apparent air of superiority about them. They talk down to you as if you are intellectually deficient and emotionally unstable. They have no pity when it

comes to showing off new targets after the breakup, guaranteeing that you see how delighted they are without you.

27. **Double-crossing chatter that changes on an impulse.** They plant seeds of poison, whispering about everybody, idealizing them to their face, and then grumbling about them behind their backs. You discover yourself doing not like or resenting people you've never even met. For some reason, you might even feel unique for being the one she or he complains to. Once the relationship turns sour, they'll run back to everybody they insulted to you, lamenting about how crazy you've become.

28. **Your feelings**. Your natural love and empathy have transformed into overwhelming panic and anxiety. You say sorry and weep more than you ever have in your life. You barely sleep, and you wake up every early morning feeling distressed and unhinged. You have no idea what happened to your old unwinded, loveable, easygoing self. After an altercation with a toxic person, you will feel outrageous, exhausted, tired, stunned, and empty. You tear apart your entire

life-- spending cash, ending friendships, and searching for some sort of reason behind everything.

You will discover that regular, caring people do not raise any of these flags. After an encounter with toxic people, the majority of survivors deal with the struggle of hypervigilance: Who can be relied on? Your gauge will swing back and forth for a while, like an unstable pendulum. You will question if you've gone mad-- wanting to think the best in an old friend or a new date, but feeling sick to your stomach when you invest time with them because you're waiting on the manipulative habits to begin.

Establishing your instinct is a personal procedure, but I would leave you with this: the world is primarily complete of good people, and you don't want to miss out on that since you've been injured. Spend some time contacting your feelings. Keep tweaking until you find a comfortable balance between awareness and trust. Look within and comprehend why you felt the way you did when you were with your abusive partner and how you felt before you met them. You will find that many old relationships may need revisiting. And as you start to abandon toxic patterns, healthier ones will undoubtedly appear in their place.

To estimate a longtime member and friend, Phoenix, you will stop asking, "Do they like me?" and start asking, "Do I like them?"

What Is Normal?

If your "soul mate" went from captivated to bored in the blink of an eye, this is not normal. If you were called envious and crazy by somebody who actively cheated on you, this is not normal. This is not normal if you are left desperately waiting by your phone for texts on regular basis.

When this person is gone from your life, you will discover that everything starts to make good sense once again. The commotion dissolves, and your peace of mind returns. Things will be normal once again.

Beware of the Vultures

You are taking the first steps to recuperate from a toxic relationship with a narcissist. That's fantastic! The work you'll be doing will not just totally free you from the grasp of your abuser, but it will likewise enable you to reclaim yourself-- the self that was squashed on, beaten down, and changed into a shell of who you once were. I know it may be challenging to face some of the realities we'll be exploring, but it's also empowering, as you'll see how much you've made it through, how strong you indeed are.

As you begin this work, I strongly encourage you to look for a recovery professional or a healing community. You'll need the support and, at times, an encouraging reminder that you're on the right course.

Its crucial to note that after repeated abuse, you're going to be vulnerable and exceptionally raw. As you start to put the pieces together, you'll feel devastated, miserable, and angry. It's frustrating.

You're most likely used to repressing your emotions and dealing with things by yourself. However, this time, everything is not in the open. You're dependent like a newborn child, looking for someone-- anyone-- to understand what you're going through.

In basic, it's essential to be open with your feelings. At your most insecure moments, you might unknowingly open the floodgates for more abuse.

It's no secret that survivors appear to draw in more unreasonable people like magnets. As you frantically share your story, you latch on to the quickest and most sympathetic ear-- anyone who proclaims to knows you. The issue is, these people do not always have your interest in mind.

Those happy to listen to your demented story for hours on end are, sadly, not likely to be people who have purchased your healing.

They are more than likely "vultures".

Vultures frequently seem exceptionally kind and warm. They want to fix you and absorb your problems. They are fascinated by your struggles. But eventually, you will find yourself lost in another headache. They begin drowning you in unsolicited advice. They need consistent appreciation and attention. You are not allowed to disagree with them. They feed off drama, and a pressing need to be appreciated by others.

You will find that they snap as you end up being happier. They view your development as a risk to their control. They wish to keep you in a continuous state of reliance. They do not want you to look for assistance from anyone except them.

Whether these people are narcissists or not, you do not require this toxic trash after what you've been through.

Its advisable that all survivors should avoid looking for new friendships and relationships for at least a couple of months. You should define where you no longer need-- or desire-- to speak about your abuser any longer.

Stick to professional treatment or healing communities and services when you need assistance. These people understand what you've been through, and you're going to discover that all of them want to help-- with no strings connected.

I know the temptation to go out and meet new people. You're looking to start rebuilding your life. You desire to surround yourself with kinder and more genuine good friends. And you will. But genuine friends won't be acting as your therapist, and they absolutely will not be babbling on about their ability to emphasize and care.

It takes a long time to begin developing healthier relationships. It takes breaking old routines, forming new ones, establishing your instinct, and lastly, about understanding what it is that you want from this world.

Be on the lookout for vultures. In the composing world, there's a world rule called "show-- don't tell." This rule also uses to people. If you experience somebody who's continuously telling you who they are, just how much they wish to help you, how they will make things right for you, take a step back and look at their actual habits. Manipulative people are always "saying" because they have nothing good to show. Their unethical and inappropriate actions never match up with their right words, causing an overwhelming cognitive dissonance in the people who trust them.

You will discover that good, humble people aren't trying to tell you who they are and what they can do for you. They just show it through consistent love and generosity. A" shower" will only share their point of view without trying to twist the conversation in their favor. Avoid those who tell you how good they are, how generous they are, how effective they are, how sincere they are, and how important they are. Instead, search for the quiet ones who show these qualities every day through their actions.

Toxic people condition us to disregard our instinct, and we need to find out to trust it again. Instead of judging outwardly, we need to assess secretly. When we start focusing on our feelings, this is where the recovery begins. And if you are focused, we can agree on this simple truth: great people make you feel good and bad people make you feel bad. Everything else forms from there.

Don't listen to the people who say your feeling need to be completely independent of the world around you. If you've got an open heart, that's difficult. As humans, we have this incredible gift-- the ability to make another person feel fantastic with a word or a soft smile. It's what makes the world attractive. Some people would call this love.

You experienced an abuser, someone who controlled this present to cause discomfort. And now you have to avoid people like this so it'll never happen again.

Think about someone you love. Someone who regularly inspires and never disappoints, It could be anybody-- your mama, a friend, your children, your cat, a deceased relative. Truly, anybody. You might feel that you have no Constant. Naturally, you do; you can even dream one up. Imagine a greater power in your mind-- one that brings peace to your heart. Vibrant, blooming, and full of life, embodying all the qualities you admire most: empathy, compassion, kindness—a gentle spirit who will always keep you safe. And voilà, you have a Constant.

With time, you will start to discover the people who make you feel bad. You realize that you do not need to endure negativity when there is a Constant who brings out the best in you.

Once you end up being more comfortable with the idea, you'll be ready to ask the essential question of all: Shouldn't I feel this same kind of peace with everyone in my life?

Absolutely. Yes.

CHAPTER EIGHT

Learning How to Recover From Emotional Abuse and Increase Self Esteem

When dealing with narcissists, one of the problems that most people encounter is that they can frequently be unjust and so unreasonable. From the narcissist's point of view, the world should revolve exclusively around him. This chapter offers some concepts on how you can begin to set limitations on the narcissist's behavior and develop better personal boundaries.

At times it might seem like the narcissist has taken over your every awakening minute or envelops your every idea and feeling. Keep in mind; a real narcissist is very proficient at representing himself as being the center of the universe; he is truly good at making you feel that your purpose in life is to serve him. Why? Because he thinks that he is exceptionally distinct, skilled, and unique and that you are not. What's often amazing is how once his power is eliminated, or he is exposed or disarmed, he no longer appears to have the same hold over others. This is frequently true of playground bullies. As long as their peer's quake in fear as the bully approaches, he will have unbelievable power over his schoolmates, but as soon as someone withstands him, the tide changes relatively rapidly.

We're not recommending that you wrestle your narcissist to the ground and begin pounding him (however appealing this might be). Instead, what we will have you explore are ways in which you can withstand the narcissist, so you are no longer bullied into doing things that you do not wish to do or that you might feel obligated to do.

Valuing Yourself and Increasing Your Self-Worth

One of the starting points for setting limitations is being able to accept that you have rights too. It's easy to feel that you don't count or don't matter if you've been dealing with a narcissist for any considerable length of time. After a while, you may get brainwashed into thinking that the narcissist is the only one who matters and that you are just along for the ride. Jan Black and Greg Enns (1997) make the point that boundary setting is not so much a matter of mastering unique methods or appealing expressions to use as it is a matter of implementing a feeling of how you should be treated.

What you can change in your life begins with your self-worth. Valuing yourself and developing a greater sense of your worth will not happen magically but rather will come from practice and collective effort. Keep in mind; it's alright to put yourself first.

How to Boost Your Self-Worth

Jan Black and Greg Enns (1997) list several ways to value yourself more. Some of the suggestions include:

- Make decisions that are about you, options that will support your self-worth, such as doing more activities that are self-encouraging.
- Acknowledge your worries and what causes your stress and anxiety, but try to challenge these fears. Do not let them get

the best of you. If you're anxious about flying, try to challenge your worry by flying to a place you will take pleasure in or have never been to before.

- Recognize your preferences, whether they are eating certain foods or doing certain leisure activities, such as going to the films, pursuing artistic hobbies, or reading books, and plan time to enjoy what you like.
- Embellish your home, apartment, condominium, or office in manner ins, which you find pleasing. Use pictures or images that are your, which help to assert that this is your area.

When you're having a difficult time making choices, pretend you're providing guidance to your friend. What would you recommend to your friend?

- Imagine your objectives. Where would you like to be a month from now, three months from now, six months, or a year? Imagine how you will be and how you will be different.

As you evaluate this list, could you imagine yourself following some of these actions? Which do you feel would be simpler for you to achieve? Which would be harder for you? It would be practical to analyze what you think might hold you back if some actions look like they would be more challenging.

Empowering Yourself by Setting Boundaries

Asserting yourself and asking that your needs be met will give you a much better chance of being heard; at least, the narcissist might respect your determination to stick up for yourself.

You may want to take time to consider the kinds of situations where the narcissist in your life does things that trouble or frustrate you. Does she make demeaning remarks about you (about your look or something you like)? Does he always say things that are created to draw attention to himself, or does he boast about real or imagined achievements? Does she make jokes at your expenditure? Does he spend an excessive quantity of time on his look? Is she insensitive to your needs? Is he indifferent to what you believe or feel? If the narcissist is in your work environment, does this person take credit for your work?

Does she exploit you for her gain or well-being? Does he make little needs of your time or effort?

To set limits on these habits, you must begin to consider ways you can react that are different from how you might usually react. It just makes sense that "If you wish to feel something you've never felt before, you should want to do something you've never done before." You will have to think about trying a different way if what you've been doing isn't working.

Learn to Say No

The very first thing you'll need to do is include the word "No" to your dictionary. If you have tried to set limits with the narcissist and were not successful in the past, you will need to be patient. If you are firm enough, you can set limits. Here are some examples of how to react:

Narcissist: Could you take care of my pitbull for the weekend? I'm going to camp with my friends.

You: No!

Narcissist: I'm short of cash. Could you lend me $200?

You: No!

Narcissist: I'd like you to come to work over the weekend to get some reports done.

You: No, I can't. I've already made plans and will be away this weekend.

Narcissist: Could you take my mother to the doctor? I have another appointment.

You: No. I have a meeting that day as well.

Narcissist: But I can't take her. You'll need to change your appointment.

You: No, I'm busy that day.

Stick to Your Guns

It's essential to remember that in sticking to your guns, you are only repeating what you've told the narcissist. There's no need to come up with a great excuse. No means, no! You don't need to explain yourself, though sometimes it may be helpful to emphasize that you're unwilling or unable to do what's being told to do. If you're having a tough time saying no, imagine if the situation were reversed: if the narcissist was refusing to do something that you've requested of him, would he give you an explanation? Think about it.

It's important not to succumb to risks or intimidation (such as the risk of being rejected a raise or suggestion). The narcissist will take a yard if you give an inch. As Sandy Hotchkiss (2002) explains, the operative word when setting boundaries is control, meaning that you are in control. Remember, narcissists are usually used to being in control and getting others to do their bidding, so at first, it may seem somewhat unusual for you to take control and set the limits.

Another way to set limits on narcissistic behavior is to recognize those behaviors that you are no longer going to endure. You can write a statement or declaration that you are no longer ready to tolerate these behaviors any longer. This personal statement of self-reliance is your declaration of borders; it's not meant to be shown, anyone. A lot more critical than jotting down what you will no longer endure is succeeding through it. Remember, actions speak louder than voices.

CHAPTER NINE

How Narcissist/Toxic Relationships Affect You

With time, you'll begin to ask your friend as the truth of their personality might start to show through the fractures. They're no longer right, and they might seem unreasonable, challenging, and at times, even toxic to be with, which they are. Because of your preliminary belief of them, you may find it challenging to come to terms with reality.

What's more, you've already seen what takes place to people who might get on their wrong side. Because the majority of your loved ones are theirs as well, you might be forced to avoid fights to protect your image from their onslaught and hostility.

Typically, you wish to stay away from narcissists at all costs because it's challenging to leave their web once you're tangled. So, keeping these tips in mind when dealing with new people can assist you in determining narcissistic tendencies before you're in deep.

However, what about the people that you can't choose? What about those who have stayed in your life for a while, but you've just got to recognize they are narcissists? How do you deal with them, and is it possible to keep them in your life without ruining your relationships and your credibility?

Dealing with Narcissists

There is a usual saying that says prevention is better than cure, which is confirmed when dealing with narcissists. If you now know how to find them, your primary objective ought to be to keep them at arm's length. Avoiding them from working their way into your life can save you energy and keep you from having to bend over backward to satisfy and please them.

On the other hand, there are examples when avoidance isn't a viable choice. Family relations can't be chosen, and are generally long-term engagements that you can't quickly get rid of. Because of how they've become implanted in your life, childhood friends that turn out to be narcissistic grownups are also hard to deal with.

While it might be mentally and emotionally draining to work away from the bonds you've developed with narcissists, it's possible. And you might even have the ability to do it without making a big scene. But before you go through the process, here are a few things you need to keep in mind when trying to clear away the energy vampires in your life:

- **They're Not Likely to Change**

However, what if they are a better person? Everyone should have a second chance. One of the reasons people tend to find it challenging to cut a narcissist out is because of the idea that people change. While it holds that people can change, you need to comprehend the context that narcissists live in.

These people turn down criticism, believe they're always right, and aggressively defend their position against anybody, despite their relationship to that person. They merely hate being told that they're wrong in any way, and they will fight violently to make sure that they get things their way.

With feeble insight about what they do and how they act, it's tough to take advantage of a narcissist and make them see the reality of their life or their behavior. That's why those who experience the character condition and those with extreme tendencies rarely ever voluntarily seek therapy and treatment.

When it comes to it, anybody who attempts to point out their flaws is just jealous. It's impossible for these people to change, no matter how many members of their family and their friends, you're able to meet up to serve the truth.

All that said, you should not expect a narcissist to change. If they reveal signs of modification, it's most likely not to change at all, but a tactic to get you to soften up and then abuse you once again with their managing, oppressive need for supremacy and affection.

- **You Will Look Bad**

While it's possible to cut bonds with a narcissist while handling little damage, you have to know that there is no such thing as a neat exit approach. This is especially true if you share more relationships like friends, members of the family, and colleagues with the narcissist you wish to break off with.

For example, a man who grew up with a narcissistic father might try to restrict his interactions with his moms and dad to give himself some freedom to move, live, and decide for himself. His youth friend who grew up knowing his daddy might ask and discover the distance, "Why don't you visit your daddy anymore?"

Explaining his reality might help him launch suppressed feelings. But because his friend matured just scratching the surface of his father's personality by sharing light discussion, seeing him at the family house, and hearing stories about him from other people, he might think the child is unreasonable and rash.

"He's the only daddy you'll ever have." Sure, that is real. From another person's point of view who's been sapped of energy all his life, it looks like a small price to pay.

Keep in mind, a lot of people around you matured in well-adjusted houses with good friends, family members, and moms and dads who likely weren't narcissistic. So, they will not be able to feel sorry for you because they do not know what it's like to handle somebody with narcissistic propensities.

Above that, you might also incur a couple of scratches to your image because of the narcissist's natural tendency to drop tricks to other people. Once they observe what you're trying to do, or if your try to break it ends in an explosive argument, be prepared to manage the seclusion.

Narcissists will divide and conquer, scratching you out of the image and persuading all your classic friends and family members to believe the worst about you. This means that some of the most crucial people in your life may cut you out as well, because of the nasty stories that might start spreading out soon after you break off the relationship.

- **It's Going to Hurt**

This eventually depends on the depth of your relationship with the narcissist, but in many cases, it can be unpleasant to work away those knots that bind you together. If it's been years since you became a part of each other's lives can be a psychological journey, finding that somebody is a narcissist mainly.

It takes a lot of effort and time to unwind all the layers of their personality, and you might be surprised when former realities are all of a sudden exposed to be absolute lies. A kid who when believed that his mom's and dad's limiting nature was well-meaning, might be surprised to find out that it was an exercise of control.

As you go through the procedure and unpack more and more of the facts in front of you that weren't obvious at the beginning, you may feel embarrassment, anger, and betrayal. Do not stress-- it's all part of the recovery. Simply keep your head high and advise yourself that none of their behaviors define who you are as a person.

- **Can You Live with Them?**

Can you think of entirely separating yourself from someone you've known and loved for several years? How about someone who you considered to be a part of yourself, like a romantic partner or a family member? No doubt, dealing with even just the idea of losing somebody you love out of your volition might look too tough to bear - even if that person makes you feel bad about yourself and the world around you. Many end up asking - is it possible to live with a narcissist?

For those people who do not wish to cause discomfort on others or withstand pain themselves, there's the option of merely suffering through the emotional, mental, and possibly even physical abuse. This is generally seen as the 'simple escape' because it gets rid of the need for conflict, and hence lessens the possibilities of ruining relationships. If you're significantly invested in the relationship you have with a specific narcissist, then the idea of leaving might not even cross your mind at all.

- **Is it truly that easy?**

When you think about things from the perspective of the now, you might state that avoiding a narcissist can only trigger more harm. Still, the opposite is real—called energy vampires, keeping these harmful people around you might eat your mental and psychological health. They can make you question yourself and force you to put your needs on hold.

Over the long run, you might find yourself having a hard time and sputtering to keep a smile on your face. You might be fearful of their criticism and their explosive temper. People who stay in narcissistic relationships all their lives declare a feeling of loss of identity and have been reported to manifest early indications of anxiety.

What you have to know is that while it may seem perfect to just 'neglect' their habits and preserve your presence in each others' lives instead of cutting them out completely, their practices will make them difficult to be with down the line. As people, there's only a lot we can take, and you need to know that your energy is restricted. When that vampire saps you dry, then you'll begin to experience burn out.

What does a person look like after years of suffering through a narcissist's abuse? Here's a sneak peek at the possibilities:

-Devoid of an independent identity.

Narcissists yearn for control and will do anything and everything they can to make sure people near them manifest the qualities and potentials they believe deserve praise. Of course, if you're going to be closely associated with them, you have to look and act in a particular way so they will not feel 'embarrassed' to have you hanging around.

Their unreasonable desire for perfection will create impractical expectations for people around them. If these expectations are not met, then they turn to criticizing and insulting the person who failed them.

If you're picking to stay, then you have to know how this can affect your identity. Victims of narcissistic abuse discover themselves always living in stress and anxiety and worry, wondering when the next explosive episode might happen. Not wishing to be the reason for it, they send themselves to the desires of the narcissist.

-This mentality of 'peace at all cost' jeopardizes the person's identity.

They have to dress, act, and react the way the narcissist wants them to, causing them to quit their unique preferences and qualities. Over the long run, a victim may entirely lose his or herself, unable to make decisions without first talking with the narcissist for approval.

-The function of the scapegoat.

If you've chosen to deal with a narcissist, then you need to be ready to be their scapegoat. These people will feel upset and angry most of the time, and it often doesn't truly matter who did what - they'll lash out at anyone within the environment.

For you, this means potentially taking the force for a variety of issues that weren't even your fault, to begin with. The narcissist might use that as fuel to validate their anger on you if you made even just a minor mistake within the same time frame.

So a spouse who just overcooks her narcissistic spouse's dinner a bit more than he wants may find him unreasonably chewing her out after a stressful, difficult day at work.

In these situations, your best defense would be to say you're sorry. Yes, even if you were not at fault. You need to embrace the role of the placator - the person who simply does whatever their narcissistic partner desires to maintain peace.

-Varying treatment.

Today, the narcissist loves you. Tomorrow, they hate you with a burning passion. The way a narcissist treats you will not be set in stone, and they can flip that switch almost instantly depending on a range of factors.

Narcissists know that the people around them want their approval and love because it's tough to come across. They will intentionally control people by giving and taking their love whenever they see it needed. If you act opposite to what they want, then the narcissist will keep all care and love up until you come to your senses and act according to their preferences.

- **A painful lack of empathy**.

Imagine going to a family gathering with your narcissistic partner. Throughout the festivities, as everybody enjoys the food and business, one of the visitors brings up their recent promotion. Not wishing to let the conversation dwell too far from herself, the narcissist rifles through her mind to find something she can talk about- related to the topic but with enough substance to make her look good.

She chooses to talk about the report you provided at work, which tanked. Your employers were unimpressed and asked you to recreate the whole thing, which your partner shares as if making a joke. To top everything off, she ends the story with "I tried to tell him what to do, but he just does not listen!"

She looks good, you look bad, and how she managed to get people to ask her questions about her story, allowing her to keep all eyes on her. She wins. But you? You're left sitting in the corner, shaking your head in shame.

A narcissist wouldn't know what empathy was even if it ran them over. They can't 'put themselves in others' shoes' and just see things how they wish to. In many ways, you can liken them to a horse with blinders on - they can't see anywhere around them, just what's in front of them.

Living with a narcissist means suffering through the embarrassment and humiliation that comes hand in hand with their need for attention. They will exploit your tricks even if you're right there to hear them do it, as long as it means having the ability to keep the spotlight for a little longer.

- **Exploiting your unique vulnerabilities.**

Perhaps among the hardest things to deal with when you continue to deal with the energy vampire in your life is their method of exploiting distinct vulnerabilities. They know where it hurts, and they'll jab their finger into that open injury if it means showing you that they're distraught at you.

Narcissists will rely on the vilest, upsetting, and immoral tactics if it means rubbing salt into their victim's open wounds. They will not think twice about hitting you where it hurts, and they'll likely do it even if it might be incredibly challenging to fix or challenging to reverse.

- **A separated life.**

When you choose to stick to a narcissist, you cross out everybody else in your life. You end up being an extension of the toxic person, and therefore you are technically his or her property. So your commitment belongs to them, and you can't just hang around with people you want to be with because they feel it compromises their control.

On top of that, the narcissist also separates you to manage what you show other people. Being among a couple of who's conscious of who the narcissist is behind closed doors, they'll wish to make sure that you do not end up spilling the beans and making them look harmful to people you might know.

One of the first things they will do is bad mouth you to your closest family and pals if you end up in an argument with the narcissist. They'll play the victim and act as though you worked out of percentage and reason, earning them the sympathy of the parties they're trying to appeal to.

Once they have that secured, they'll caution these people that you're ' dangerous,' 'unstable,' and 'untrustworthy.' This creates a bias and preempts any attempts you might make to speak about your recent run-in with the narcissist. When you choose to share what you've been through, the closest people in your life already have some idea - albeit askew - as to what happened. Therefore your story might not sell.

Typically, you'll have to tread this lonely road all by yourself. And you have to be ready to be left by a few of the essential people in your life if you happen to make the error of arguing with the narcissist.

Now, it's worth asking - is it worth it to keep a narcissist in your life? Usually, people who choose to preserve the presence of an energy vampire battle to see the truth. They continue believing that the initial impression the narcissist provided is who they are, which this painful behavior is simply a stage.

What you need to remember is that narcissism is never a stage - it's a way of life. That initial impression was a necessary action in their scheme to find victims and keep them where they are. By showing you something great at the beginning, you're enticed into this toxic relationship, and the narcissist wins at discovering their supply.

Leaving the narcissist is always the most intelligent thing to do. You need to think about your well-being and mental health. Sometimes, you will need to endure fight and discomfort, but if it's in your best interest, then it may be worth it. Just keep in mind to keep your emotional health above everything, and secure your energy from those who look to suck you dry and damage your sense of self.

CHAPTER TEN

How you Can Deal with Toxic People

The recovery process is the start of your new life. You'll recall old characteristics, questioning how you ever endured such toxicity. You might even feel ashamed about your previous habits. This regret is your self-respect beginning, suggesting that you're different now.

After the relationship, you find yourself "cheerleading" a lot, distributing compliments as a way to receive them back yourself. You may especially do this with other abuse victims. With time, your compliments will start to be far more personal and sincere. You develop strong friendships with people whom you care about, instead of just selflessly throwing yourself at every survivor you meet along the way. This is healthy. The world is a prominent place. You should not be friends with everybody you come across. It's far much better to have a couple of buddies than a million acquaintances with whom you exchange shallow formalities.

Along those same lines, survivors who spend their days supporting other abuse victims need to take pride in themselves. Whether it be online, in person, or over the phone, you're doing something extraordinary to change the world. Abuse healing is a part of who you are, and you ought to be comfortable sharing this with friends and partners. You work with survivors, which is a passion worth cultivating.

As you become your most genuine self, the people around you will not-so-coincidentally begin to change. Enjoy this, and don't forget to credit yourself for all of the efforts you've made to make it a reality.

Finding the Beauty, You've Always Had

Paradoxically, the horrific injury that is left by the toxic people will allow the victim to do better. It will take some time and numerous stumbles, but themselves see the substantial beauty within themselves later. If they give it time, they will see themselves as the perfect person, and feel a great sense of fitting. They can then rejoice in their own uniqueness! That charm is inside every survivor, a beauty we have possessed all along and never knew we had. As you progress your journey through your recovery process, you have the power to get the beauty within by seeing and accepting the following realities:

- **You were not silly; you were innocent.**

When you first recognized the level of the narcissist's betrayal, you most likely were overwhelmed by pity. How is it that you overlooked the status of the lies and the control? It is typical to be so dumb when reality sinks in. And it is easy to be upset with yourself for not knowing that the "love" the psychopath used you was an impression. This is how the narcissist (master of deception) wants you to feel, yet it is not the fact! You are a loving, empathetic person. You were never taught that emotionally crippled human predators are out there; you only found out about them in fairy stories or stories of serial killers. You did not know that they walk amongst us, a lot of them look familiar, law-abiding people. You cannot safeguard yourself from something that you never understood existed.

- **It is all right to have vulnerabilities and insecurities.**

You have probably been warned that it is "bad" to be insecure or susceptible. You might even be taught this by those who are attempting to help you recover from emotional abuse. Struggling with insecurities and being vulnerable with others is part of what makes you a typical human being. Even the most positive people question themselves at times; even the most emotionally healthy people need to open up their hearts to others and become susceptible if they wish to build intimate, significant relationships. You can get new self-confidence and still keep the ability to permit others-- the perfect others-- into your inner circle. Your strengths and weaknesses were used.

You might feel that the methods which the narcissist used you just display your drawbacks.

You might think that you have unique issues that make you a narcissist magnet. You were too trusting; you lacked limits; you did not love yourself enough, and so on. It is real that your weak points were exploited. However, your strengths were also used.

The ability to love is a strength.

The ability to trust is a strength.

The ability to comply is a strength.

The ability to be honest and kind, and compassionate is a strength.

A narcissist has no conscience, and because of that, he or she can see horrific ruthlessness. She or he uses pity plays to gain from your natural desire to offer generosity and understanding. The narcissist mirrors your values and all elements of your personality-- including your positive qualities-- to make you think that he or she is like you when she or he is the opposite.

The narcissist sets you up in a way that you project your happiness on him or her.

CONCLUSION

Narcissists in a relationship are energy vampires-- they'll make you feel like you owe them the world, including your sense of self-esteem, self-confidence, and security. They'll make every day a sophisticated obstacle to navigate with care. Make the wrong turn, and you might be face to face with their demons.

Just like the typical image of pop culture vampires over the years, real-life energy vampires can be sexy, exceptional, pleasant, and charismatic. They discharge a beauty that pleads to be praised, and we just can't help but give them the attention that they so obviously should have at a look.

It's because of their exceptional capability to give themselves in the best way possible that makes it simple for the rest of us to feel captivated and fall in love. We gravitate towards them; we give ourselves completely to them; we try to be a part of their life because we want that perfection to rub off on us. When the smoke clears, and the mask is pulled off, the real narcissist reveals its actual nature.

Behind closed doors, these people can be the worst to deal with. They'll make you feel like everything is your fault, and they'll make you question your abilities and skills. They will destroy your reputation and your relationships without thinking twice, and they'll laugh at you when it's all over. They'll manage you and take your identity; they'll want you to toe a tight line and whip you back in shape when you make the tiniest lousy move.

They're difficult to handle, and they're not yours to fix. At the end of the day, the narcissist in your life will not change. Accept that. Don't think that it was ever your responsibility to make them a better person. It never was. What you need to think about is your self-respect, your psychological health, and your emotional well-being.

You are your responsibility, and you need to safeguard yourself from the vampires around you.

Take this information as your wooden stake and drive it through the heart of the relationship you've been trying to save. Before anybody else, protect yourself from the abuse and provide yourself the possibility at a much better life and much better relationships. There are many people out there who would gladly give you what you should have without any strings attached.

Is it possible to live life without the abuser you've come to know and love? No. Remember, you can't put it from an empty vessel. Restore yourself first and remove the people who sap you of what you have to give. This should be able to help you find your way to more fruitful, more loving relationships that will reciprocate the affection and positivity you have to share.

CPSIA information can be obtained
at www.ICGtesting.com
Printed in the USA
LVHW011944241020
669606LV00012BA/570

9 781801 114004